Adelmann of Liège
and the Eucharistic Controversy

DALLAS MEDIEVAL TEXTS AND TRANSLATIONS

EDITOR
Philipp W. Rosemann
(University of Dallas)

EDITORIAL BOARD

Jeremy du Quesnay Adams (Southern Methodist University); David L. Balás, O.Cist. (University of Dallas); Denis M. Farkasfalvy, O.Cist. (University of Dallas); Theresa Kenney (University of Dallas); James J. Lehrberger, O.Cist. (University of Dallas); J. Stephen Maddux (University of Dallas); John R. Sommerfeldt (University of Dallas); Francis R. Swietek (University of Dallas); Bonnie Wheeler (Southern Methodist University)

BOARD OF EDITORIAL ADVISERS

Charles S. F. Burnett (Warburg Institute); Marcia L. Colish (Yale University); Thérèse-Anne Druart (Catholic University of America); Kent Emery, Jr. (University of Notre Dame); Bernard McGinn (University of Chicago); James McEvoy (†); James J. Murphy (University of California, Davis); John T. Noonan, Jr. (U.S. Court of Appeals for the Ninth Circuit, San Francisco); Edward M. Peters (University of Pennsylvania); Carlos Steel (Katholieke Universiteit Leuven); Baudouin van den Abeele (Université catholique de Louvain); Nancy van Deusen (Claremont Graduate University).

SPONSORED BY

UNIVERSITY OF DALLAS

DALLAS MEDIEVAL TEXTS AND TRANSLATIONS
16

Adelmann of Liège and the Eucharistic Controversy

BY

Hans Geybels
(Katholieke Universiteit Leuven)

With a musicological study of the *Rhythmus alphabeticus*
by Pieter Mannaerts (Katholieke Universiteit Leuven)

PEETERS
PARIS - LEUVEN - WALPOLE, MA
2013

Cover illustration: King Edward's vision of Christ during the elevation of the host, an illumination in MS. Cambridge, University Library, Ee.3.59, fol. 21r. This famous manuscript, produced in the 1250s at Westminster Abbey, contains the only known copy of the Anglo-Norman *La Estoire de Seint Aedward le Rei*, a versified hagiographical text most likely authored by Matthew Paris. By kind permission of Cambridge University Library.

A catalogue record for this book is available from the Library of Congress.

© 2013 – Peeters – Bondgenotenlaan 153 – B-3000 Leuven – Belgium.
ISBN 978-90-429-2682-0
D/2013/0602/13

All rights reserved. No part of this publication may be reproduced, stored in a retrieval system or transmitted, in any form or by any means, electronic, mechanical, photocopying, recording, or otherwise, without the prior written permission of the publisher.

UT IN OMNIBUS GLORIFICETUR DEUS

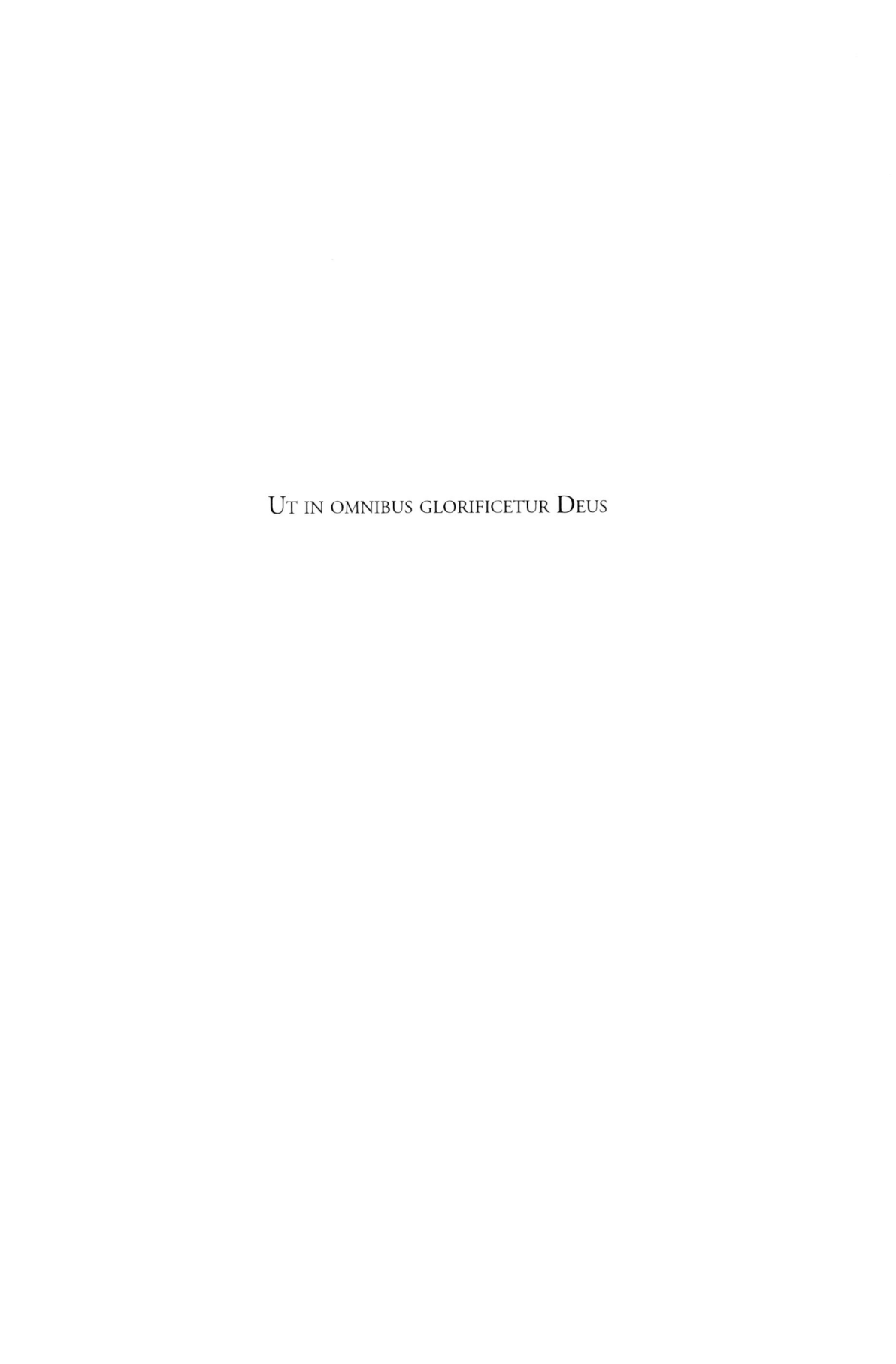

MS. Brussels, *Koninklijke Bibliotheek van België*, 5576–604, fol. 163r. The top part of the folio contains the end of Berengar's letter to Adelmann; on the sixth line from the bottom, the words, "Mitto etiam" indicate the beginning of Adelmann's *Rhythmus alphabeticus*. Note also, on line seven from the bottom, the words, "Aulus mannus," Berengar's ironic designation of Adelmann as "Aulus the pony." By kind permission of the Royal Library of Belgium.

Editor's Foreword

Launched in 2002, the Dallas Medieval Texts and Translations series pursues an ambitious goal: to build a library of medieval Latin texts, with English translations, from the period roughly between 500 and 1500, which will represent the whole breadth and variety of medieval civilization. Thus, the series is open to all subjects and genres, ranging from poetry and history through philosophy, theology, and rhetoric to treatises on natural science. It will include, as well, medieval Latin versions of Arabic and Hebrew works. Placing these texts side by side, rather than dividing them in terms of the boundaries of contemporary academic disciplines, will, we hope, contribute to a better understanding of the complex coherence and interrelatedness of the many facets of medieval written culture.

In consultation with our distinguished board of editorial advisers, we have established principles that will guide the progress of the series. The primary purpose of the Dallas Medieval Texts and Translations is to render medieval Latin texts accessible in authoritative modern English translations; at the same time, the series strives to provide reliable Latin texts. The translations are therefore established either on the basis of existing good critical editions (which we will reprint, if possible) or, when necessary, on the basis of new editions. These will usually be semi-critical, with an apparatus limited to important variants. Each volume comprises scholarly introductions, notes, and annotated bibliographies.

Works published in the Dallas Medieval Texts and Translations are unexcerpted and unabridged. In the case of a work too long to appear in a single volume, we will start with the beginning of the work or publish integral parts of it, rather than creating an anthology of discontinuous texts.

* * *

Adelmann of Liège, to whose works this sixteenth volume of the series is devoted, is not a well-known medieval theologian. In many of the standard works of reference (such as the *Lexikon des Mittelalters*) one will look in vain for an entry on him. Yet, as Professor Geybels argues, both Adelmann and the school of Liège to which he belonged played an important role in the second Eucharistic controversy, which occurred in the eleventh century. Berengar of Tours believed that the consecration amounted to an "assumption" of the Body and Blood of Christ by the Eucharistic bread and wine; moreover, he maintained that Christ resides in the *res sacramenti*,

the "reality" of the sacraments, but not in the sacraments as such (which, he argued following Augustine, are mere figures and signs). Against this theory of a school that they graphically termed *impanatores*, the Liégeois attempted to formulate a pre-scholastic version of the dogma of transubstantiation: at the consecration, the substances of bread and wine change into the substances of the Body and Blood of Christ.

These points emerge very clearly from the correspondence between Adelmann and Berengar which Professor Geybels has beautifully translated for us and elucidated with learned commentary. Adelmann's letter to Hermann II, bishop of Cologne, throws light on a related aspect of the Liégeois position: in each sacrament—whether it be the Eucharist or penance, the subject matter of the letter to Hermann—Christ Himself is at work. No priest can say, "I forgive you your sins" because it is God alone who forgives sins and justifies the sinner. Adelmann is scandalized, therefore, at the practice of casually pronouncing sins forgiven as part of regular Eucharistic celebrations.

The *Rhythmus alphabeticus*, published here in its two known versions, rounds out this edition and translation of the complete works of Adelmann of Liège by allowing us to catch a more personal glimpse of Adelmann as a playful composer of verses (and, in one of the versions, music) about some of his contemporaries.

* * *

As usual, I conclude this foreword with thanks to the University of Dallas, whose continuing financial support makes this series possible. Our publisher, Peeters of Leuven, deserves gratitude for taking on the series, and for producing it in such an attractive format. Finally, thanks are due to the medievalists in the United States and abroad who have agreed to serve on our board of editorial advisers or to assess individual manuscript submissions.

Philipp W. Rosemann
January, 2012

Table of Contents

Editor's Foreword	vii
Acknowledgments	xi
Preface	1
Pre-Scholastic Views on the Sacraments in the School of Liège (Adelmann and Alger)	5
Adelmann of Liège's Life	37
Introduction to the Texts, including	41
The Neumes of Adelmann's *Armonice facultatis* in the Copenhagen Manuscript (by Pieter Mannaerts)	56
Letter from Adelmann to Berengar	62
Letter from Berengar to Adelmann	82
Letter from Adelmann to Hermann II of Cologne	96
Rhythmus alphabeticus	104
Notes	117
Bibliography	125
Indices	135

Acknowledgments

Thanks are due to the following individuals and institutions for graciously allowing us to reprint earlier editions of the Latin texts translated in this volume:

— Brepols Publishers, of Turnhout, granted us permission to use two letters by Adelmann—to Berengar and Hermann II of Cologne, respectively—which Professor R. B. C. Huygens edited recently for Corpus Christianorum, Continuatio Mediaevalis, vol. 171.
— Father Marcel Haverals, editor of the series "Spicilegium sacrum Lovaniense," gave us permission to reprint the edition of Berengar's letter to Adelmann that Jean de Montclos included in his 1971 study, *Lanfranc et Bérenger. La controverse eucharistique au XIe siècle*.

Thanks are returned, as well, to the libraries that have provided images of manuscripts from their collections, allowing us to reproduce them in this volume: the Cambridge University Library, the *Koninklijke Bibliotheek van België* in Brussels, and the *Kongelige Bibliotek* of Copenhagen.

Preface

In his 1264 encyclical *Transiturus de hoc mundo* Pope Urban (1261–1264) ordered that the feast of Corpus Christi (called *festum sanctissimi corporis Christi*, and since the liturgical reform of Vatican II, *festum sanctissimi corporis et sanguinis Christi*) be held in the entire Roman Catholic Church on the second Thursday after Pentecost (the Thursday after Trinity Sunday) to celebrate the true presence of the Body and Blood of Christ in the Eucharist. The feast was even accorded an octave and, although that is now abolished, the feast itself is still prominent. In honor of the new holiday, the pope requested that Thomas Aquinas write an office, *Sacerdos in aeternum*, which contains the famous hymn, *Pange, lingua, gloriosi Corporis mysterium* ("Sing, my tongue, the glorious mystery of the Body").[1] The feast of Corpus Christi is just one of the many expressions of Eucharistic piety that have survived to the present day; it is still popular and even an official holiday in many parts of the world. The most familiar custom on that day is the Procession of the Blessed Sacrament, featuring the devotion to the consecrated host (in some rare cases also to the consecrated wine).

The origins of this feast can be traced, indirectly, to women's pious circles (such as the Beguines and the Cistercian nuns) from the beginning of the thirteenth century in Brabant and Liège. They displayed an unusual interest in the real presence (*praesentia realis*). That interest developed under the influence of the writings of Bernard of Clairvaux and William of Saint-Thierry, who emphasized the feeling of unification with Christ. This mystical union can be achieved through union with Christ in the Eucharist, since it is in the Eucharist that Christ gives himself totally. There can be either a real reception of the communion or some form of spiritual communication. Since that time, the veneration of the Sacrament became part of the ritual of spiritual communion. Whether the communication happens in actuality or spiritually is of minor importance, since the Sacrament is first and foremost spiritual sustenance and hence intended primarily for the salvation of the soul. Therefore, medieval Eucharistic piety can best be described as follows: in order to gain eternal salvation a certain kind of union with Christ is necessary. That union

---

[1] See Pierre-Marie Gy, "L'office du Corpus Christi et S. Thomas d'Aquin. État d'une recherche," *Revue des sciences philosophiques et théologiques* 64 (1980): 491–507. The best and most recent overview in English is Barbara R. Walters, Vincent Corrigan, and Peter T. Ricketts, *The Feast of Corpus Christi* (University Park, Pa.: The Pennsylvania State University Press, 2006).

can be achieved through the Sacrament, which owes its effect to Christ's sacrifice on the Cross.[2]

The immediate motivation for installing the feast of Corpus Christi was a local celebration based on the visions of the Augustinian nun Juliana of Mont-Cornillon († 1258). She repeatedly saw a moon disk with a piece missing from the rim, a vision that she interpreted to mean that there was a feast missing from the Church: one to celebrate the gift of the Eucharist. It might be true that without Juliana, the Church would have never known the feast of Corpus Christi, but the standard historic account tends to ignore the fact that she was part of a longer tradition. In fact, this tradition began in the School of Liège. Indeed, when Robert of Thourotte, bishop of Liège from 1240 to 1246, introduced the feast of Corpus Christi in his diocese, he relied directly on the writings of Adelmann of Liège.[3]

Thus, the recognition of the Feast of Corpus Christi was preceded by sustained theological debates on the nature of the Eucharist. As Miri Rubin explains:

> It is interesting to note how many rather basic eucharistic issues had remained only loosely formulated until the eleventh century[:] [t]he nature of sacramental change, the nature of Christ's presence, the moment of transformation, the symbolic link between matter and God. ... Basic questions like concomitance and transubstantiation were still open; similarly, the nature of communion and frequency of celebration were issues which were regulated by local customs and which, by and large, were not at the centre of pastoral interest.[4]

Adelmann of Liège must be seen in the context of what is generally known as the "second Eucharistic controversy," which took place in the eleventh century. The first controversy, between Paschasius Radbertus and Ratramnus, dates back to Carolingian times.[5] The second dispute was between Berengar of Tours on one side and, on the other, Adelmann, Alger of Liège, and Lanfranc of Bec. After this conflict, the Catholic Church officially adopted what later became known as the doctrine of real presence. Peter Lombard and Thomas Aquinas were the primary thinkers to refine this important dogma until it received its final definition of transubstantiation during the Council of Trent.

---

[2] See Charles Caspers, *De eucharistische vroomheid en het feest van Sacramentsdag in de Nederlanden tijdens de Late Middeleeuwen*, Miscellanea Neerlandica 5 (Louvain: Peeters, 1992), 12.

[3] See ibid., 265.

[4] Miri Rubin, *Corpus Christi: The Eucharist in Late Medieval Culture* (Cambridge: Cambridge University Press, 1999), 14 and 24. Gary Macy has written a brilliant survey of the theological debates in this early scholastic period; see Gary Macy, *The Theologies of the Eucharist in the Early Scholastic Period: A Study of the Salvific Function of the Sacrament according to the Theologians c. 1080–c.1220* (Oxford: Clarendon Press, 1984), esp. chap. 2: "The Paschasian Approach to the Eucharist" (pp. 44–72).

[5] See Peter Browe, *Die Eucharistie im Mittelalter. Liturgiehistorische Forschungen in kulturwissenschaftlicher Absicht*, Vergessene Theologen 1 (Münster: LIT, 2003).

It appears, then, that the sacramental devotion that existed in popular circles had an "elitist" origin. The intense interest in the Eucharist developed by the theologians of the tenth and eleventh centuries slowly trickled down into the general religious population, until in the middle of the thirteenth century it culminated in the figure of Juliana of Mont-Cornillon. Historians tend to be exclusively interested in the activities of these pious communities, and easily lose sight of the theological origins of Eucharistic piety. But it is no coincidence that Liège was the center of Eucharistic devotion; for it was in precisely this region that the most advanced theological reflection on the Eucharist took place. The two most famous scholars who wrote on this subject were, without a doubt, Adelmann of Liège and especially Alger of Liège, both of whom were members of the renowned cathedral school of Saint-Lambert ("the Athens of the North") at the time of the peak of its excellence.[6]

* * *

The present volume contains all the hitherto discovered writings by Adelmann of Liège: an extensive letter from Adelmann to Berengar (Berengar's response is also included), a fairly long letter to abbot Hermann, and a poem. Especially the first two texts (Adelmann's letter and Berengar's response) are very important for documenting the Eucharistic controversy. The other texts are mainly of historical value: in the letter to Hermann a disciplinary question is discussed, the song contains a list of the masters of the time, and the poem is an ode to a student.

Adelmann was surely not the most important interlocutor of Berengar of Tours in the second Eucharistic controversy, but being—as far as we know—the first to criticize Berengar, he remains worth reading. Only recently, yet another "minor theologian" in this controversy has been rediscovered, namely, Alberic of Monte Cassino.[7] Both Adelmann and Alberic hold a realistic view of the presence of Christ in the bread and wine, stressing the identity of sacrament and matter. Berengar, however, refuses to adhere to that Platonist-Augustinian explanation. He relies on logic and reason when he states in his *Rescriptum* that "by consecration at the altar

---

[6] On the cathedral school, see Jean-Louis Kupper, *Liège et l'église impériale (XIe–XIIe siècles)*, Bibliothèque de la Faculté de Philosophie et Lettres de l'Université de Liège 228 (Paris: Les Belles Lettres, 1981), esp. 311–51 and 375–83. On the later period, see Christine Renardy, *Le monde des maîtres universitaires du diocèse de Liège 1140–1350. Recherches sur sa composition et ses activités*, Bibliothèque de la Faculté de Philosophie et Lettres de l'Université de Liège 227 (Paris: Les Belles Lettres, 1979), and eadem, *Les maîtres universitaires du diocèse de Liège. Répertoire biographique 1140–1350*, Bibliothèque de la Faculté de Philosophie et Lettres de l'Université de Liège 232 (Paris: Belles Lettres, 1981).
[7] See Charles M. Radding and Francis Newton, *Theology, Rhetoric, and Politics in the Eucharistic Controversy, 1078–1079: Alberic of Monte Cassino against Berengar of Tours* (New York: Columbia University Press, 2003).

the bread and wine are made into religious sacraments, not so that they cease to be that which they were, but so that they are that which is changed into something else, as the blessed Ambrose says in his book On Sacraments."[8] The debate could be reduced to two questions: "If the body of Christ is naturally present, why is it not sensed? How can the Fathers speak of a presence in sign (*in sacramento*) if the reality itself is present?"[9]

These were important (and dangerous) questions indeed. Edward J. Kilmartin clarifies the meaning of Berengar for the history of Eucharistic theology in the following words:

> Since the time of Berengar, and largely because of the controversy associated with his eucharistic teaching, the following questions have been explicitly asked by theologians: (1) What are bread and wine? (2) What changes take place with the bread and wine? (3) How is the change to be conceived? (4) When does the change take place? (5) By what instrumental cause does the change take place?[10]

The debate began when Adelmann wrote to Berengar to ask for some clarifications of his position. Adelmann had heard that Berengar defended a view according to which the body and blood in the Eucharist were not the true body and blood of Christ, but only a kind of figure and likeness. Adelmann was rather surprised. He was of the opinion that this issue had long been settled …[11]

---

[8] Translation ibid., 11.
[9] These two questions are from Macy, *The Theologies of the Eucharist*, 46.
[10] Edward J. Kilmartin, *The Eucharist in the West: History and Theology*, ed. Robert J. Daly (Collegeville, Minn.: The Liturgical Press, 2004), 98.
[11] See Radding and Newton, *Theology, Rhetoric, and Politics in the Eucharistic Controversy*, 16.

Pre-Scholastic Views on the Sacraments in the School of Liège

In the early Middle Ages there were two prevailing definitions of the sacraments by two different authors: Augustine and Isidore of Seville. In some early works (*De magistro* and *De doctrina christiana*), Augustine had described a sacrament as the exterior and visible sign of a sacred reality. The famous definition is contained in the phrase, *sacramentum, id est sacrum signum*.[1] Another well-known and often repeated Augustinian definition was, *Sacramentum est invisibilis gratiae visibili forma*.[2] For the Bishop of Hippo, *sacramentum* is almost identical with *mysterium*, that is, the visible manifestation of God's saving presence in Christ and the Church, through which men participate in the divine mystery. Augustine discovered many examples of sacraments in the Old as well as in the New Testament: rituals, feasts, historical events, sacred places, and so on.[3]

Less than two centuries later, Isidore, in his *Etymologiae*, defined a sacrament as a material thing referring to a spiritual reality; moreover, the sacrament not only refers to the spiritual reality, but also serves as its envelope and a support.[4] The

---

[1] Augustine, *De civitate Dei* 10.5, ed. Bernardus Dombart and Alphonsus Kalb, CCSL 47 (Turnhout: Brepols, 1955), 277$^{15-16}$.

[2] Augustine, *Quaestionum in heptateuchum libri septem* 84, ed. Iohannes Fraipont, CCSL 33 (Turnhout: Brepols, 1958), 228$^{1886-7}$.

[3] For Augustine (and also etymologically) a sacrament is a thing that makes something else sacred: Jesus' crucifixion, circumcision, a temple, the Our Father, the imposition of hands, etc. For a comprehensive overview, see Emmanuel J. Cutrone, "Sacraments," in *Augustine Through the Ages: An Encyclopedia*, ed. Allan D. Fitzgerald (Grand Rapids, Mich.: Eerdmans, 1999), 741–7.

[4] See Isidore of Seville, *Etymologiae* VI.xix.39–43, ed. W. M. Lindsay (Oxford: Clarendon Press, 1911): "Sacramentum est in aliqua celebratione, cum res gesta ita fit ut aliquid significare intelligatur, quod sancte accipiendum est. Sunt autem sacramenta baptismum et chrisma, corpus et sanguis [Domini]. Quae ob id sacramenta dicuntur, quia sub tegumento corporalium rerum virtus divina secretius salutem eorundem sacramentorum operatur; unde et a secretis virtutibus vel a sacris sacramenta dicuntur. Quae ideo fructuose penes Ecclesiam fiunt, quia sanctus in ea manens Spiritus eundem sacramentorum latenter operatur effectum. Vnde, seu per bonos seu per malos ministros intra Dei Ecclesiam dispensentur, tamen quia sanctus Spiritus mystice illa vivificat, qui quondam Apostolico in tempore visibilibus apparebat operibus, nec bonorum meritis dispensatorum amplificantur haec dona, nec malorum adtenuantur, quia (1 Cor. 3, 7): 'neque qui plantat est aliquid, neque qui rigat, sed qui incrementum dat, Deus'; unde et Graece mysterium dicitur, quod secretam et reconditam habet dispositionem."

difference between the two definitions became particularly clear in the case of the Eucharist. For both, this sacrament consisted in the consecration of bread and wine, but for Augustine bread and wine were to Christ as *signum* is to *signatum*, whereas Isidore identified bread and wine with the Body and Blood of Christ.[5]

Theologians of the early Middle Ages (roughly before 1050) by and large preferred the version of Isidore; thus in the ninth-century Eucharistic quarrel between Paschasius Radbertus and Ratramnus, both parties accepted Isidore's definition. From around 1050 onward, this attitude changed when Berengar showed much more interest in the Augustinian definition since Isidore's definition did not correspond well with his own conception of the Eucharist. Berengar, well aware of Augustine's standing, was so eager to defend the Augustinian concept of sacrament that he made a collation of seven definitions formulated by Augustine. The list is preserved in his letter addressed to Adelmann.[6] From the eleventh century the two main Augustinian definitions became more and more important because, via Berengar, they were promoted by Lanfranc of Bec, Ivo of Chartres, and Peter Abelard. Of course, authors such as Lanfranc and Yves believed that they represented the orthodox interpretation of the phrase, *sacramentum sacrum signum*.[7]

To summarize: in the period before Alger and Adelmann, theology did not utilize a single and clear definition of sacrament; apparently, no need was felt to present a systematic sacramentology. Theologians used the two Augustinian definitions and offered two different interpretations, namely, a realistic and figurative one. Only in the twelfth century was the concept of sacrament modified and, in the process, rendered more precise.[8] Isidore's generic definition of a sacrament, applicable to all the rites of the liturgy, became more and more limited. The eleventh-century debates on the nature of the sacrament of the Eucharist—that is, the change of the substances of bread and wine into the substances of the Body and Blood of Christ— were crucial for this evolution.

---

[5] See Damien Van den Eynde, *Les définitions des sacrements pendant la première période de la théologie scolastique (1050–1240)* (Rome: Antonianum; Louvain: Nauwelaerts, 1950), 3–4 and 8.

[6] See "Letter from Berengar to Adelmann," in this volume, pp. 86–95. The letter is studied in Josef Geiselmann, *Die Eucharistielehre der Vorscholastik*, Forschungen zur christlichen Literatur- und Dogmengeschichte 15 (Paderborn: Schöningh, 1926), 293–5. In *De sacra coena* 44, Berengar offers an eighth definition; see Berengar of Tours, *De sacra coena adversus Lanfrancum*, ed. W. H. Beekenkamp, Kerkhistorische studiën 2 (The Hague: Nijhoff, 1941), 150. Four of these definitions were constantly to be reproduced in scholastic treatises (see Van den Eynde, *Les définitions des sacrements*, 16).

[7] Abelard promoted the other definition (*invisibilis gratiae visibile signum*); see Van den Eynde, *Les définitions des sacrements*, 8–10.

[8] See ibid., 18–31.

Pre-Scholastic Views on the Sacraments in the School of Liège

The theological school of Liège was renowned in the eleventh century (being called *flos Galliae* and *alter Athena*[9]), but it has unfortunately received little scholarly attention. It was a Liège theologian who started the controversy with Berengar.[10] The theologians of Liège played a significant role in the disputes concerning the Eucharist. Here we will first discuss the meaning of some crucial concepts (*sacramentum*, *figura*, and *modus significandi*) in the works of Adelmann (ca. 1000–ca. 1061) and Alger (ca. 1060–1131), two leading representatives of the school of Liège.[11] Since the available documentation informs us far better on Alger, we will devote most of our attention to him. Thereafter, we will study the contributions of both to the development of sacramentology. Their sacramentology appears in high relief in their discussions with Berengar, and within the framework of the Gregorian reform.[12] In the following texts, one must pay attention to the fact that the term "sacrament" was not yet defined rigorously in the later, scholastic manner.

Sacramentum

Let us begin with an excerpt from Alger's *De sacramentis corporis et sanguinis Dominici* on the concept of sacrament:

Quid sit sacramentum, et quot modis accipiatur.	What is a sacrament, and in how many modes is it received?
Quia igitur hoc suo sacramento Christus Ecclesiam suam unit sibi et concorporat, de	Because Christ, through his sacrament, unites his Church with himself and becomes one

---

[9] Gozechinus, *Epistola ad Walcherum*, ed. R. B. C. Huygens, CCCM 62 (Turnhout: Brepols, 1985), 15$^{133-4}$.
[10] Theoduin of Liège sent a letter accusing Berengar to King Henry I of France; see *Epistola contra Brunonem et Berengarium*, PL 146:1439–42.
[11] Alger was of particular importance for pre-scholastic theology, not only because of his treatise on the Eucharist, but mainly because of his work on canon law, *De misericordia et iustitia*. As Robert Kretzschmar writes, "Die Bedeutung des Werkes als Quelle für die Geschichte des Kirchenrechts und das Zeitalter des Investiturstreits ist unbestritten: Es zählt zu den unmittelbaren Vorlagen, die Gratian bei der Abfassung seiner Concordia discordantium canonum heranzog, und stellt fraglos ein hervorragendes Dokument der gedanklichen Auseinandersetzungen dar, von denen die Zeit der gregorianischen Reform geprägt war" (*Alger von Lüttichs Traktat "De misericordia et iustitia". Ein kanonistischer Konkordanzversuch aus der Zeit des Investiturstreits. Untersuchungen und Edition*, Quellen und Forschungen zum Recht im Mittelalter 2 [Sigmaringen: Jan Thorbecke Verlag, 1985], ix). See also the first chapter of Charles M. Radding and Francis Newton, *Theology, Rhetoric, and Politics in the Eucharistic Controversy, 1078–1079* (New York: Columbia University Press, 2003).
[12] See, for example, Edward J. Kilmartin and Robert J. Daly, *The Eucharist in the West: History and Theology* (Collegeville, Minn.: The Liturgical Press, 1999).

veritate ejus et virtute, quasi de re ineffabili, quantum Deus dederit disseramus: si tamen prius quid sacramentum sit discutientes, quomodo figura a veritate rei quam significat, discernenda sit ostenderimus. Augustinus in libro X De civitate Dei (c. 5): "Sacramentum visibile, invisibilis rei sacramentum est, id est sacrum signum." Item Augustinus in lib. II (c. 1, t. III, c. 19) De doctrina Christiana: "Signum est res praeter speciem quam ingerit sensibus, aliud aliquid ex se faciens in cognitionem venire." Item alibi (Quaest. in Levit. 84): "Sacramentum est invisibilis gratiae visibili forma."

Sciendum autem quod sacramentum et mysterium in hoc differunt, quia sacramentum signum est visibile aliquid significans, mysterium vero aliquid occultum ab eo significatum. Alterum tamen pro altero ponitur, ut superius dictum est: mysterium vestrum accipitis, ut sit mysterium occultans et occultum, et sacramentum signans et signatum. Unde Maximus in quadam homilia Epiphaniae (hom. 10): "Mystica ejus nativitas sempiterno gaudio et terram laetificavit et coelum. Hunc ergo regem coelestium, hominumque rectorem sub carnis mysterio venientem, impius tremit Herodes." Nec solummodo sacramentum pro alterutro, id est, vel pro signo vel pro signato invenitur, sed etiam pro utroque. Sicut cum dicitur: Verbum caro factum est (Joan. I, 15), caro pro carne et anima. Itemque: Omnis anima potestatibus sublimioribus subdita sit (Rom. XIII, 1): anima pro carne et anima accipitur. Nec mirum, si sacramentum pro sacramento et re sacramenti saepius ponitur; quia et corpus Christi pro sacramento et corpore Christi invenitur. Augustinus, De sacramentis altaris: "Corpus Christi, et veritas et figura est. Veritas, dum corpus

Body with it, we will—to the extent that God allows it—examine this reality and effect as if we deal with an ineffable *res*. However, we will show that we first have to define a sacrament and how a figure must be distinguished from the reality of the *res* that it signifies. Augustine says in the tenth book of *The City of God*: "The visible sacrament is the sacrament of an invisible *res*, that is, a sacred sign." Further on, Augustine writes in the second book of *On Christian Doctrine*: "A sign is indeed a *res* that, more than effecting an impression on the senses, produces out of itself another idea in the mind." And elsewhere: "A sacrament is the visible form of invisible grace."

One has to distinguish sacrament and mystery, because the former is a sign signifying something visible, while a mystery signifies something hidden. Occasionally the one is taken for the other, as we said above. You accept your mystery as if it is a concealing and concealed mystery, and a sacrament as if it is a signifying and signified sacrament. Therefore, in a homily on Epiphany, Maximus writes: "His mystical birth delighted both heaven and earth with an eternal joy. The impious Herod fears this heavenly king, this leader of men who comes under the mystery of the flesh." *Sacrament* has been invented not only for either sign or signified, but also for both at the same time. For example, when it is said, "The Word became truly flesh (*caro*)," in this case, *caro* means "flesh" as well as "soul." Similarly: "Each soul is subordinate to supreme powers." In this case, *anima* is considered to be both flesh and soul.

No less remarkable is the fact that *sacrament* means both the sacrament and the matter (*res*) of the sacrament, because *Body of Christ*, too, is used for the sacrament as well as for the Body of Christ. Augustine explains in *On the Sacrament of the Altar*: "The Body of

Christi et sanguis, virtute Spiritus in verbo ipsius, ex panis vinique substantia efficitur. Figura vero est, id quod exterius sentitur."

Sciendum etiam quod sacramentum in sacris codicibus non semper pro sacro signo, sed sacramentum aliquando jusjurandum, aliquando res sacrata accipitur. Unde Ambrosius in libro ad Gratianum apparuisse dicit hominibus unigenitum Patris per sacramentum assumpti hominis, quasi diceret: Per hominem quem sibi sacravit, quia homo non signum, sed potius occultatio divinitatis fuit.[13]

Christ is reality as well as figure. It is a reality since the Body and Blood of Christ are brought about out of the substance of bread and wine through the power of the Holy Spirit in his word. What is externally perceived, however, is the figure."

Nevertheless, one should also know that in the sacred codices the word *sacrament* does not always designate a sacred sign, but sometimes an oath, sometimes a consecrated *res*. Therefore, in his book to Gratian, Ambrose writes that the first-born of the Father appeared to humanity through the sacrament of assumed humanity, as if he were saying: "It is through the human being whom he consecrated to Himself that He appeared to humanity, because the human being was no sign, but rather a concealment of the divine."

Alger answers the question regarding the essence of a sacrament with Augustine's famous definition: *Sacrificium ergo uisibile inuisibilis sacrificii sacramentum, id est sacrum signum est*, "a visible sacrifice, then, is the sacrament of an invisible one, that is, a sacred sign."[14] Berengar and contemporaries such as Lanfranc and Guitmond of Aversa reproduced the Augustinian definition.[15] According to this definition, a

---

[13] Alger, *De sacramentis corporis et sanguinis Dominici*, PL 180:751^{B15}–752 ^{B6}. A better edition of this treatise is an important desideratum.

[14] Augustine, *De civitate Dei* 10.5 (see note 1); also see *Contra adversarium legis et prophetarum* 2, ed. Klaus-D. Daur, CCSL 49 (Turnhout: Brepols, 1985), 119$^{993-7}$: "Ita ne uero ubi essent cognoscenda tantae rei sacramenta, id est, sacra signa et in re pudenda atque in eis uerbis, quibus uerecundia debetur, cognosci non debuisse nec dici, homo iste sciebat et beatus apostolus nesciebat?" Note the difference between Augustine's original definition and Alger's changes. Alger writes, "Sacramentum visibile, invisibilis rei sacramentum est, id est sacrum signum." Augustine speaks of *sacrificium*, Alger talks of *mysterium*. Alger adds to this: "Sacramentum signum est visibile aliquid significans, mysterium vero aliquid occultum ab eo significatum" (*De sacramentis*, 751^{D2-4}). There is a tendency to frame a sacrament as something that is both *signum* and *signatum*.

[15] See Berengar, *Rescriptum contra Lanfrannum*, ed. R. B. C. Huygens, CCCM 84 (Turnhout: Brepols, 1988), 193$^{166-8}$: "In eodem: Sacrificium ergo visibile invisibilis sacrificii sacramentum, id est sacrum signum, est." Lanfranc, in *De corpore et sanguine Domini* (PL 150:422^{C2-4}), writes: "Et nos sacramentum, de quo agimus, sacrum esse signum credimus, et credendum suademus." It is in his letter to Adelmann that Berengar sums up six Augustinian definitions of a sacrament. For Guitmond's definition, see Guitmond of Aversa, *De corporis et sanguinis Domini veritate*, PL 149:1457^{D1-2}: "Vocatur enim sacramentum, id est, sacrum signum."

sacrament is not an outward sign of inward grace, instituted by Christ to sanctify mankind, but rather something that signifies or represents an invisible reality.[16] This is the main reason why, in the title of his treatise, Alger speaks of the "sacraments" (plural) of the Body and Blood of Christ.[17] In the Eucharist the species of bread and wine are the sacraments since, thanks to these species, faith recognizes the presence of the Lord on the altar.

One problem is the definition of a sacrament; another is the application of this definition to the Eucharist. What is the *sacrum signum* of the Eucharist? After all, in a pre-scholastic context a sacred sign can signify a variety of things. Lanfranc mentions only a few, such as "sacramentum Dominicae passionis, divinae propitiationis, concordiae et unitatis, postremo assumptae de Virgine carnis et sanguinis."[18] Alger prepares the scholastic position by emphasizing the Body of Christ.[19] The sacrament is considered to reside in the material elements, namely, the visible species of bread and wine. The subsisting species of bread and wine are the *sacramenta* of the Body and Blood of Christ, which are the *res sacramenti* that remain invisible. The species are the sacrament, but the Eucharist is a sacrament as well, because it signifies an invisible reality.

The greatest difference of opinion with Berengar concerned the meaning of the Body of Christ. Alger agreed with Lanfranc's position, taking the Body of Christ to be the Body which was born from the Virgin Mary and immolated at Calvary.[20] Christ substantially had but one Body, but his Eucharistic Body was the sacrament of his historical Body.[21] For Berengar, the species were simply signs, and he was

---

[16] See Alger, *De sacramentis*, PL 180:752^{B10-C6}.

[17] Migne's edition is slightly deceptive, in that it uses *De sacramentis* in the general title of the edition, while the header is always *De sacramento*.

[18] Lanfranc, *De sacramentis*, PL 150:415^{A12-14}. Guitmond emphasizes the passion (Guitmond of Aversa, *De corporis et sanguinis Domini veritate*, PL 149:1457^{B3}).

[19] See Alger, *De sacramentis*, PL 180:752^{B14-C6}: "Formam panis et vini et caeteras elementorum remanentes et visibiles qualitates, sacramentum tantummodo vere dici et esse; substantiam autem illam invisibilem, quae ipso sacramento operta est et in quam panis et vini substantia translata est, vere et proprie dici et esse corpus Christi ...."

[20] See ibid., 792^{D4-10}: "Caro ejus [= Christi] est, quam, forma panis opertam, in sacramento accipimus, et sanguis ejus, quem sub vini specie et sapore potamus; caro videlicet carnis, et sanguis sacramentum sanguinis. Carne et sanguine, utroque invisibili, intelligibili, spirituali, significatur Redemptoris corpus visibile et palpabile: plenum gratia omnium virtutum, et divina majestate." Alger thinks that he is quoting from Prosper of Aquitaine's *Liber sententiarum Prosperi* (a collection of "sentences" from the works of Augustine), but actually it is Lanfranc's *Liber de corpore et sanguine Domini* (PL 150:423^{D14}–424^{A5}).

[21] In the Berengarian controversy, the meaning of "Body of Christ" is crucial. Berengar made the Eucharistic Body a sacrament of the historical Body of Christ. The orthodox theologians emphasized the substantial identity between the two Bodies. This question is further analyzed in Jean de Montclos,

right in using Augustine to prove his point of view. The problem, however, was that the meaning of sacrament had evolved and that the Augustinian definition represented an older strand of doctrine in sacramentology.

In *De misericordia et iustitia*, Alger draws a clear distinction between *sacramentum* (the visible sign), *res sacramenti* (the present Christ), and *effectus sacramenti* (later called *res tantum*, that is, the grace infused into the soul of the communicant). Alger needs this distinction because he wants to demarcate the sacrament as visible sign from the invisible spiritual grace that it signifies. This distinction was to become crucial in scholastic sacramental theology.[22]

Apart from the *signum*-definition of sacrament, Alger also repeats the second one derived from Augustine, which Berengar also used: *Sacramentum est invisibilis gratiae visibili forma*. Note that Alger equates *forma* and *signum*, seeing no difference between the terms. Abelard does: a sacrament is a sign rather than a form, and it is a sign of nothing other than a non-sensible *res* which consists in supernatural grace.[23] It is also important that he changes the phrase *sacramentum sacrum signum* into *sacramentum sacrae rei signum*.[24] It seems that Alger is not sufficiently aware of what this modification implies, but for Abelard the difference matters. Alger would consider this just a grammarian's splitting of hairs, but for Abelard such details go to the heart of the matter. Here we observe a clear distinction between Alger's Carolingian methodology and Abelard's dialectical approach.

The difference between pre-scholastic and scholastic conceptions of sign and sacrament will become even clearer if we focus on the scholastic theory of the sign. In scholastic theology, too (for example, Peter Lombard), a sacrament is a *signum sacrum*. A sign is the *res*—beyond the species that bears upon the senses—which

---

Lanfranc et Bérenger: la controverse eucharistique du XIe siècle, Spicilegium sacrum Lovaniense. Études et documents 37 (Louvain: Spicilegium Sacrum Lovaniense, 1971), 383–91. Alger deals with this matter in chapter 18 of the first book of *De sacramentis* (PL 180:792^{A1}–794^{A4}: "Quod invisibile corpus Christi in sacramento, sacramentum sit visibilis corporis Christi in humana forma, verum veri, idem ejusdem." He devotes many words to the substantial presence of Christ in the Eucharist (see ibid., 815^{A13}–821^{B13}.

[22] See Alger, *De misericordia et iustitia*, PL 180:884^{D6-14}/Kretzschmar, *Alger von Lüttichs Traktat "De misericordia et iustitia,"* 235: "In quo notandum est et credendum, quia, cum sacramenta alia tantum duo in se contineant, sacramentum scilicet et effectum sacramenti; istud solum tria sacramentum, speciem illam, scilicet que videtur, rem sacramenti, id est veritatem dominice substantie, que, sicut de Virgine vere nata est, vera in ea esse creditur; effectum sacramenti, quo quibusdam ad vitam, quibusdam ad iudicium sumitur" [ed. Kretzschmar].

[23] See Peter Abelard, *Theologia 'scholarium'*, ed. E. M. Buytaert and Constant J. Mews, CCCM 13 (Turnhout: Brepols, 1987), 321–66, no. 119.

[24] Ibid., 321$^{90-4}$.

causes something else outside of itself to enter into the mind.[25] Peter Lombard spends a whole paragraph particularly on the distinction between sign and sacrament. A sacrament is in the first place the visible form of invisible grace (*invisibilis gratiae visibilis forma*). Some signs are natural (like smoke signifying fire), others are given and, of the latter, some are sacraments, some are not. This means that every sacrament is a sign, but not the other way around. Every sacrament bears the likeness of the reality that it signifies. If sacraments did not have this likeness, they could not properly be called sacraments. A sacrament is properly said to be a sign of God's grace and the form of invisible grace; it bears its image and exists because of it. Therefore, sacraments have not only been instituted for the purpose of signifying, but also of sanctifying. Those things that only have been instituted for signifying are just signs, and not sacraments.[26]

Figura

Quod sacramentum duobus modis significat, vel sua ex se similitudine, vel alicujus actionis erga se.	A sacrament can signify something in two ways: through similitude with the reality it signifies or through similarity of an external action upon it.
Sua ex se similitudine sacramentum significat, sicut cum Dominus dicit: Caro mea vere est cibus, et sanguis meus vere est potus; et: Ego sum panis vivus qui de coelo descendi (Joan. VI, 55); quia, sicut cibus et potus temporalem vitam, sic ipse dat aeternam. Unde ait: Si quis manducaverit ex hoc pane, vivet in aeternum (ibid.). Et merito. Si enim tanta vis est in cibo qui non vivit, nec manet, ut labentem vitam hujus temporis foveat et retineat quandiu Deo placuerit, quanto magis Christus cibus vivens immortaliter, vitam aeternam conferre credendus est, quibus	A sacrament signifies something through similitude with the reality it signifies when the Lord says: "My flesh is truly food, my blood is truly drink," and: "I am the living bread which has descended from heaven." In the same way in which food and drink sustain temporal life, He sustains eternal life. Therefore He says: "If someone will eat this bread, he will live forever." And rightly so. If there is so much power in food that does not live nor persevere, that it can preserve and promote the perishable life of these days—as much as it will please God—then it is all the more believable that Christ, the eternally living

---

[25] See Peter Lombard, *Sententiae in IV libris distinctae* IV, dist. 1, cap. 3 (Grottaferrata: Collegium S. Bonaventurae ad Claras Aquas, 1971–1981), 2:233: "Augustinus, De doctrina christiana: Signum vero est res, praeter speciem quam ingerit sensibus, aliud aliquid ex se faciens in cogitationem venire."

[26] See ibid., cap. 4: "Sacramentum eius rei similtudinem gerit, cuius signum est.—Augustinus: Si enim sacramenta non haberent similitudinem rerum quarum sacramenta sunt, proprie sacramenta non dicerentur."

sibi placuerit? Magis enim credendus est vitam conferre, qui vitam in se habet et vita est, quam qui non habet. ...

Nec solum sua ex se similitudine cibi et potus nomine et specie, significari se voluit vitam aeternam, sed etiam ex panis et vini similitudine significari voluit aliud corpus suum, id est Ecclesiam. Unde Augustinus in sermone De sacramentis fidelium, feria II Paschae: "Quia passus est pro nobis, commendavit nobis in isto sacramento corpus et sanguinem suum, quod etiam fecit nos ipsos. Nam et nos corpus ipsius facti sumus, et misericordia ipsius quod accipimus, ipsi sumus." ... Item in sermone 26, super Joannem: "Hunc itaque cibum et potum, societatem vult intelligi corporis et membrorum suorum, quod est Ecclesiam." Et post pauca: "Hujus rei sacramentum, id est unitatis corporis et sanguinis Christi, de mensa Dominica sumitur, quibusdam ad vitam, quibusdam ad exitium; res vero ipsa cujus sacramentum est, omni homini ad vitam, nulli ad exitium, quicunque ejus particeps fuerit." ... Ecclesiasticam societatem, cibum et potum ac panem Dominicum dixit, tum quia vere satiat in aeterna beatitudine, tum quia multos in unum redigit vera charitate: quam societatem qui vere acceperit, non potest privari aeterna salute. Quia ergo sacramentum corporis Christi, ipsum Christum, vel ejus Ecclesiam sua ex se similitudine signat, videamus si similitudine alicujus exterioris actionis circa se idem faciat.

Augustinus in libro Sententiarum Prosperi: "Dum frangitur hostia, dum sanguis de calice in ora fidelium funditur, quid aliud quam Dominici corporis in cruce immolatio, ejusque sanguinis de latere effusio designatur? Ideo etiam ipse corpus suum fregit

food, conveys eternal life on those whom it pleases Him to. It is more credible that the one who carries life in himself conveys life, rather than someone who does not have it. ... Through the proper similarity of food and drink, nominally and specifically, He not only equates himself with eternal life, but through the same simile of bread and wine, He also wants to signify His other Body, that is, the Church. Therefore, Augustine writes in the sermon *On the Sacraments of the Faithful*: "Because He suffered for us, in this sacrament, which also created us, He entrusted us with His Body and Blood. Because we are made His Body, we ourselves are the mercy that we receive." ... Similarly in sermon 26 on John: "This food and this drink He intends as the union between the Body and its members, which is the Church." A few words later: "The sacrament of this *res*, that is, the union of the Body and Blood of Christ, is assumed at the table of the Lord, for some for life, for others for destruction. The *res*, however, of which it is a sacrament—all those who have participated in it will live, and none will die." ... He called "ecclesiastical society" the food, drink, and bread of the Lord, not only because it satiates in terms of eternal beatitude, but also because through genuine love, it reduces many to one. The one who truly accepts such a society cannot be denied eternal salvation. Because the sacrament of the Body of Christ itself properly signifies His Church, we must see whether the same happens through the similarity of an external action upon the sacrament.

In Prosper's *Book of Sentences*, Augustine is quoted: "When the host is broken and when the blood in the chalice is poured into the mouths of the faithful, what else is signified but the sacrifice of the Lord on the Cross? This is why He broke and delivered His Body,

et tradidit, ut signaret, quod sponte sua in passionem se frangeret et traderet pro nobis, qui solus potestatem habebat ponendi animam suam: quod etiam in altari vice sua imitantur sacerdotes, ut idem repraesentent, id est corpus Christi, sacramentum Christi et Ecclesiae per exteriorem actionem." Ait Sergius papa: "Triforme est corpus Domini, pars oblatae in calicem missa, corpus Christi quod jam resurrexit, monstrat; pars comesta, ambulans adhuc super terram; pars in altari usque ad finem missae remanens, corpus jacens in sepulcro, quia usque ad finem saeculi corpora sanctorum in sepulcris erunt." ...

Quidquid fit in officio missae, sacramentum est Christi et Ecclesiae. Unde et Augustinus in libro De Trinitate: Quia morte Domini liberati sumus, huius rei memores in edendo et bibendo carnem et sanguinem, quae pro nobis oblata sunt significamus. Quod enim corpus Christi in sacramento manibus fidelium tenetur, frangitur, dentibus atteritur, et ipsis incorporatur, significat eum in passione manibus impiorum tentum, et usque ad mortem fractum, et propter nostra scelera attritum; Ecclesiam vero, corpus suum scilicet, hujus suae passionis imitatione sibi incorporatam et conformatam. Quod ipsi Christo iam immortali et incorruptibili facto nullus putet esse indignum, si fidelium devotio hoc sibi in sacramento repraesentet, ad Dominicae passionis imitationem, quod ipse Dominus passurus fieri praecepit ad suam commemorationem: ut tantae rei memoria excitata, praesentiaeque divinae auxilio et exemplo roborata, velit et possit per ipsius gratiam quod nullatenus praesumit per suae

that it could signify that He, who was the only one empowered to release His soul, voluntarily broke Himself in the passion and handed Himself over for us. Like Him, priests imitate this on the altar, so that they might represent the same thing—namely, the Body of Christ, the sacrament of Christ and the Church—through an external action." Pope Sergius says: "The Body of Christ is of three forms: the part of the offering [i.e., the host] put in the chalice shows the Body of Christ which has already risen; the eaten part still wanders on earth; the part which remains till the end of the Eucharist shows the Body which lies in the grave, because until the end of time, the bodies of the saints will remain in their graves." ...

Whatever happens in the office of the Mass is the sacrament of Christ and of the Church. Therefore, Augustine says in his book *On the Trinity*: "Because we are saved by the death of the Lord, we, being mindful of this fact, indicate by eating and drinking of the flesh and blood those things which were sacrificed for us. The Body of Christ, in the sacrament which is held and broken in the hands of the faithful and which is crushed by their teeth and incorporated by them, signifies Him who during the passion was held tight by the hands of the impious, was broken until He died and crushed for our crimes. It also means the Church, namely, His Body which was incorporated into and conformed to Him through the imitation of His passion. No one thinks it unworthy—since Christ was made immortal and incorruptible—if the devotion of the faithful shows itself in this sacrament, for the imitation of the passion of the Lord, in the way that the Lord, who was going to suffer, Himself taught should be done in memory of Him; so that the aroused memory of those things, strengthened by the aid and example of

fragilitatis naturam. Quod enim in Christi corpore permissum est malis ad suam damnationem, nec ignominiosum visum est Deo Patri propter nostram salutem, multo magis ipsi placitum et gloriosum est, ut fidelium suorum manibus devote in sacramento frangatur, dentibus atteratur, sicut ipse praecepit, in suam commemorationem, non in veritate quidem passionis, crucifixionis, mortis, ut supra dictum est, sed significante mysterio, ut ipse quidem fractus et attritus integer permaneat, et redemptionis suae gratia omnibus divisa proficiat.[27]

divine presence, wants and can do—through His mercy—what no one supposes because of his fragile nature. Free rein was given to suffering in the Body of Christ at His condemnation, and this was not considered scandalous by God the Father, because it was for our salvation. It is even more pleasing and glorious to Him that in the sacrament He is devoutly broken by the hands of His faithful and that He is injured by their teeth, as He himself taught in commemoration of Him—not in the reality of the passion, the crucifixion, and death, as mentioned above, but in the signification of a mystery, so that He who is broken and injured, remains untouched and the distributed grace of His salvation benefits all.

Clearly *figura* is a crucial concept for understanding the pre-scholastic notion of sacrament. It is difficult to provide a precise translation. Sometimes its meaning is associated with *similitudo* or *imago* (and their synonyms). Ratramnus offers an idea of what the concept might mean: "One says of the true Body of Christ that it is true God and true man: God, born from the Father before the ages, and man, born of the Virgin Mary at the end of time. Well, these things cannot be said of the Body of Christ, which is mysteriously celebrated in the Church, that is, of the way in which the Body of Christ is known. The way we know it is through figure (*figura*) and image (*imago*), so that the object itself is known as truth."[28] Ratramnus explains that the Body of Christ is recognized only through a certain modality that resides in the figure and the image, so that the truth of the signified can be seen. A little further Ratramnus speaks of the *imago sacramenti*. An *imago* offers a resemblance (*similitudo*) of the truth. He concludes that the Church celebrates the Body and Blood of Christ as an image: "For this reason, the Body and Blood of Christ is what the Church celebrates, but as token, as image. The truth, however,

---

[27] Alger, *De sacramentis*, PL 180:794^{A6}–796^{D6}.
[28] Ratramnus, *De corpore et sanguine domini*, ed. J. N. Bakhuizen van den Brink, Verhandelingen der Koninklijke Nederlandse Akademie van Wetenschappen, Afdeling Letterkunde, Nieuwe reeks 87 (Amsterdam and London: North-Holland, 1974) 64: "De vero corpore christi dicitur quod sit verus deus, et verus homo. Deus qui ex patre deo ante saecula natus, homo qui in fine saeculi ex maria virgine genitus. Haec autem dum de corpore Christi quod in ecclesia per misterium geritur dici non possunt, secundum quendam modum corpus Christi esse cognoscitur. Et modus iste in figura est et imagine, ut veritas res ipsa sentiatur."

will obtain when neither the token nor the image, but rather the reality of the thing itself will appear."[29]

We have decided to translate *figura* as "figure." Adelmann writes in a letter to Berengar that the Eucharist is not the real Body and Blood of Christ, but a certain "figure" or resemblance: "… non esse verum corpus Christi neque verum sanguinem, sed figuram quamdam et similitudinem."[30] We use "figure" as the translation for *figura* in order to preserve Adelmann's use of the word. There is also a second reason: we wish to avoid any connotations from contemporary semiotic theories.[31]

Modus significandi

Alger still has to solve another important question: if a sacrament is a sign of something else—a visible *figura* of an invisible *res*—then how is it possible that the Body of Christ is a sign, since Christ's Body is invisible?[32] In chapter 19 of Book 1 (quoted and translated in the previous section), he answers that a sacrament can mean something in two ways:

(1) *sua ex se similitudine*: something visible can signify something invisible, of which it is a sign. This means that bread and wine signify the Body of Christ, which is truly present in the Eucharist.

(2) *similitudine alicujus exterioris actionis circa se*: an invisible reality can also be a sacrament, but only if an exterior action is exercised upon this reality. Through the evocation of certain circumstances from the past, an invisible reality can become a sign. So, remembering Christ's passion and death during the Eucharist makes Christ's immortal and invisible Body into the sacrament of Christ. This is of course a weak argumentation for dialecticians because its truth can ultimately be based only on Christ's authority. In scholastic theology, the question would be resolved in a completely

---

[29] Ibid.: "Qua de re et corpus Christi et sanguis est quod ecclesia celebrat, sed tamquam pignus, tamquam imago. Veritas vero erit cum iam nec pignus, nec imago, sed ipsius rei veritas apparebit."

[30] "Letter from Adelmann to Berengar," p. 64 in this volume.

[31] Jacob van Sluis uses the semiotic theory of Charles Sanders Pierce to interpret Berengar's sign theory; see his article, "Adelman van Luik: de eerste opponent van Berengarius van Tours," *Nederlands theologisch tijdschrift* 47 (1993): 89–106.

[32] Alger states that the reality (*veritas*) of the Body of Christ must always be shown through visible signs (*De sacramentis*, PL 180:779^{C1}–780^{C3}).

different way: not the Body and Blood of Christ, but the sensible species of bread and wine are the signs of Christ's immolation on Calvary.[33]

Some Aspects of the Role of the School of Liège in the Evolution of Sacramental Theology

(1) Ritualism?

To solve the problem of ritualism we take into consideration two excerpts from Alger's works, one belonging in the context of the Cyprianic controversies, the other in the context of baptism. Apparently the issue of the validity of the sacraments in the case of unworthy administrators—this was precisely the ancient and vexing question of Cyprianism—remained significant in Alger's day. According to Alger, a sacrament administered by an unworthy priest is spiritually fruitful if the priest acts officially in the Catholic Church (*intra Catholicam ecclesiam*). He addresses this matter in the prologue to *De sacramentis corporis et sanguinis Dominici*.[34] He agrees with Augustine, insisting that the sinfulness of a priest is never able to annul the effect of the invocation of the divine name, nor can it ever invalidate the power of the consecration, as long as the priest follows the official rite (*rite celebrare*).[35]

---

[33] See Louis Brigué, *Alger de Liège: un théologien de l'eucharistie au début du XIIe siècle* (Paris: Librairie Lecoffre, J. Gabalda & Cie, 1936), 102–03. Brigué also discusses the connection between the Eucharistic Body of Christ and the Body that is the Church (104–06).

[34] Adelmann discusses a similar question in his letter to Berengar. To Berengar's denial that a priest is able to work the miracle of the consecration, since a priest possesses no divine powers, Adelmann responds that Christ himself is at work in the administration of the sacraments: "Sed absit, quia quicumque baptizat in nomine Patris et Filii et Spiritus sancti, dignus an indignus, sanctus aut peccator, Catholicus aut hereticus, nihil interest, quoniam ministerium tantummodo illorum est, nec ab eis sed per eos, si recte loqui volumus, baptizatur. Christus igitur per manum et os sacerdotis baptizat, Christus per manum et os sacerdotis corpus suum et sanguinem creat" ("Letter from Adelmann to Berengar," p. 70 in this volume).

[35] See Alger, *De sacramentis*, PL 180:740^{C2-6}: "Alii autem gratiae Dei derogantes, dicunt sacerdotum malis meritis ita invocationem divini nominis annullari, ut eorum indigna consecratione non debeat panis in Christi carnem converti." The reason is that Christ is the true minister of the sacraments. This opinion was also held by Augustine, Paschasius Radbertus, Peter Damian, and others. Alger treats this question ibid. 840^{A-D}. The issue is further elaborated upon in chapter 2 of the third book, entitled "Quod solius Dei sit, omnia sacramenta facere semper vera et sancta quantum ad ipsum" (ibid., 833^{A13}–834^{A13}). Ibid., 843^{C4-5}, Alger attributes this principle to Jerome: "Ait Hieronymus ad Luciferianum: 'Sicut hic est qui baptizat Christus, ita hic est qui sanctificat.'" See also Alger, *De misericordia et justitia*, PL 180:942^{A12-B1}/Kretzschmar, *Alger von Lüttichs Traktat "De misericordia et iustitia,"* 331.

Quantum ad veritatem sacramenti nec a bono melius nec a malo pejus conficitur sacerdote. Quantum vero ad virtutem sacramenti et effectum pro fide et meritis sumentium datur aliis ad salutem, aliis ad judicium. ... Unde etiam eos impie agere, putantes ad faciendam et obtinendam eucharistiam tantum esse necessariam solemnem orationem, et non sacerdotum merita. Solemnis enim oratio sacerdoti sacramenti efficit veritatem; merita vero salutis ejus obtinent effectum et virtutem.[36]	Concerning the reality of the sacrament, it is not accomplished better by a good priest and worse by a bad priest. However, concerning the effect and the virtuousness of the sacrament for the faith and the merits of the recipients, some will be granted salvation, others damnation. ... Therefore, those who think that only solemn oration is necessary for celebrating and achieving a Mass and the merits of the priests are not important, act impiously. Indeed, the solemn oration of the priest brings about the reality of the sacrament, but the merit of his own salvation obtains the effect and the virtuousness.

At first sight, it seems that the validity of a sacrament depends only on the uttered *verba solemnia* of a priest within the Church, no matter whether he is sinful or not. The most important *verba* in the administration of the sacraments are the words that invoke the divine name.[37] To omit these words—especially the triune name of God—is to violate divine law: "Invocationem divini nominis in suis sacramentis annullari credere nefas est."[38] The reason why the rites, and especially the Trinitarian invocation, must be followed is that Christ instituted them.[39] Changing the words is equal to declaring oneself heretical. To avoid heresy, the liturgical rites should be performed without modification and the liturgical words

---

[36] Alger, *De misericordia et justitia*, PL 180:877[A12–16] and 877[D1–6]/Kretzschmar, *Alger von Lüttichs Traktat "De misericordia et iustitia,"* 224–5.

[37] See Alger, *De misericordia et justitia*, PL 180:932[B8–9]/Kretzschmar, *Alger von Lüttichs Traktat "De misericordia et iustitia,"* 315: "[O]mnia sacramenta, a quocumque in trinitatis nomine consecrata, sunt quantum ad se vera et sancta ..." [ed. Kretzschmar]. However, this is not true *quantum ad effectus/quantum ad virtutem*; in other words, a validly celebrated sacrament is not always a spiritually fruitful sacrament as well.

[38] Alger, *De sacramentis*, PL 180:833[B4–6] and ibid., 828[A1–3]. A little further, he writes: "[I]lli nomen Domini non invocant qui contra fidem, mutato ecclesiae ritu, hoc faciunt" (ibid., 850[C13–15]). The invocation of the triune name of God was always regarded as securing the validity of the sacrament of baptism. Alger extends this rule to all the sacraments, according to Nicholas M. Häring, "A Study in the Sacramentology of Alger of Liège," *Mediaeval Studies* 20 (1958): 41–78, at 43.

[39] See Alger, *De sacramentis*, PL 180:850[B14–C4]: "... non est sacramentum Christi, quod in errore positi contra institutionem Christi faciunt, nec est vera divini nominis invocatio, quia contra Christi praeceptum Christianae fidei periclitatur perfectio ...."

pronounced exactly.[40] This seems like formalism or ritualism. Concerning this point, however, the theological school of Liège is completely in line with Paschasius: The sacrament of the Eucharist is salvific for the believer if the priestly actions behind the altar are performed according to the prescribed rules. Word, rite, and effect are one in this mystery.

It would be unfair to accuse Alger of ritualism if he had made this statement only in the context of the Cyprianic debate, but he also stresses the use of the right words and invocations in other contexts. For example, when he treats baptism in *De misericordia et justitia*, faith has little or no influence on the validity of the sacrament. Sacramental legitimacy depends solely on the precise invocation of the divine name: "… quantum ad se bona sunt, quae ad invocationem divini nominis celebrantur …."[41] He reflects extensively upon this theme in chapter 13 of the third Book of *De sacramentis*:

Quaeritur autem, cum solemnia verba, et invocatio divini nominis tantae virtutis sint, ut omnia Ecclesiae sacramenta perficiant, si in ipsis ex industria vel negligentia proferentis aliquod erroris vitium sonet, utrum etiam tunc sacramenta rite perficiant? Unde sciendum est quia qui tacendo vel male proferendo quod debent in solemnibus verbis perfide peccant, eorum sacramenta ita damnat Ecclesia, ut ea vel pro nullis reputando iteret, vel pro imperfectis consummet; ita tamen, ut quae in eis vera sunt, agnoscat et approbet.[42]	Since the solemn words and the invocation of the divine name have such a spiritual effect (*virtus*) that they accomplish all the sacraments of the Church, the question arises as to whether the sacraments are still correctly performed if some vice or error (out of diligence or negligence) is heard in the words of the one who performs it. Therefore, it should be known that those who leave out or badly articulate words that are necessary for the solemn oration, sin perfidiously. For this reason, the Church condemns their sacraments, either by repeating those she considers to be non-existent, or by completing those she considers to be imperfect. In this way, the Church acknowledges and approves what is true in them.

---

[40] See ibid., 850[D10–A7]: "Ex Catholica Ecclesia sunt omnia sacramenta Dominica, quae sic habetis et datis quomodo habebantur et dabantur priusquam inde exiretis. In quo notandum est quia, si haereticorum sacramenta ab eo ritu mutantur quem Ecclesia instituit et obtinet, non sunt a Catholicis approbanda, quia mutata jam non sunt ecclesiastica, sed haeretica, sicut Innocentius, Pelagius, Gregorius, baptisma haereticorum quocunque Dei nomine factum refutaverunt, quia mutatum ab ecclesiastica institutione, non in nomine Trinitatis celebratum viderunt." Alger underlines this statement with Augustine's authority: "Si autem solemnia verba non mutantur, sed rite proferuntur, et ipsa exsecutio sacramenti rite perficitur, tunc haereticorum perfidia sacramenti veritatem non impedit, quia quod haeretici aliter non habent nec agunt quam vera Ecclesia, non emendatur a Catholicis, sed approbatur" (ibid., 851[A7–13]).
[41] Alger, *De misericordia et justitia*, PL 180:954[C14–D1]/Kretzschmar, *Alger von Lüttichs Traktat "De misericordia et iustitia,"* 353.
[42] Alger, *De sacramentis*, PL 180:847[C14–D10].

This does indeed smack of ritualism. Alger only accepts involuntary mistakes while the priest is administering the sacraments. It is necessary to believe in the words and to utter them as carefully as possible, so that the mind does not falter, even if the tongue errs out of carelessness. But then he nuances his statement. God pays more attention to the intentions (*intima cordis*) and faith of the one who is in charge than to external matters.[43] The sacrament remains "credible" even if some incorrect words are pronounced through carelessness, negligence, or ignorance, because God focuses on the true roots of faith and not "the flower of speech."[44] The main condition is faith.

This second move—the emphasis on intention—is a reflection of a change in cultural context, which until then had been heavily characterized by ritualism. For religious believers in the Germanic world, miracles were effected by precisely performed rituals, exact recitation of magical formulas, offerings of specific sacrifices at particular sacred places at fixed moments, etc. Miracles happened in places where heaven touched the earth (such as trees, springs, mountains, graves of saints). Today, this would be described as magic or as *das Heilighafte* (Mikoletzky), which attaches itself to persons or objects that bring about miracles.[45]

(2) Reason instead of Miracles?

Miracles occupy an important place in the medieval mind, because they demonstrate God's activity in the sublunary world. They permeate the everyday life of Christians.[46] Miracles function like signs. They are so striking that they are able to teach their audience things which they could not have envisaged without the aid of

---

[43] See ibid., 843^{B4-10}: "Constat ergo quia cum in sacramentis conficiendis, et dicendum sit, et credendum, utrumque sincere fieri oportet, maxime ne mens in fide titubet, etiamsi lingua per incuriam in sermone erret. Exteriora enim nostra non adeo pensantur a Domino, quantum cordis intima, qui in omni negotio magis examinat non quid, sed qua intentione vel fide fiat." Again Augustine is quoted to prove this statement.

[44] Ibid., 843^{D7-11}: "Si autem vel incuria, vel negligentia, vel ignorantia aliqua erroris verba inseruntur, non ideo sacramentum minus fieri credendum est; quia, ut supra dictum est, Deus interrogat verae fidei radicem, non locutionis florem."

[45] See Hanns Leo Mikoletzky, "Sinn und Art der Heiligung im frühen Mittelalter," *Mitteilungen des Instituts für Österreichische Geschichtsforschung* 57 (1949): 83–122, at 83. See also Aron Gurevich, *Medieval Popular Culture: Problems of Belief and Perception*, trans. János M. Bak and Paul A. Hollingsworth, Cambridge Studies in Oral and Literate Culture 14 (Cambridge: Cambridge University Press, 1995), and Arnold Angenendt, *Heilige und Reliquien. Die Geschichte ihres Kultes vom frühen Christentum bis zur Gegenwart* (Munich: Beck, 1994).

[46] See Benedicta Ward, *Miracles and the Medieval Mind: Theory, Record, and Event (1000–1215)*, 2nd ed. (Philadelphia: University of Pennsylvania Press, 1987), 1–2.

a miracle. Since Augustine's *On Christian Doctrine*, miracles were considered to be God's principal means of communication with man. Of course, they were regarded as inferior to the Scriptures, but they did complement God's teaching by means of the word. In the Scriptures, we read that God himself used miracles to stir up or to surprise His people. Through his *Dialogues*, Gregory the Great made miracles and wonder-workers (saints) extremely popular. For Gregory, miracles serve a twofold purpose: they teach faith, and they inspire men to lead a good life.[47]

Popular miracles (albeit not the biblical ones) played a relatively minor role for the school of Liège in its defense of the truth of the Body and Blood of Christ. This was a change from earlier treatises on the subject. For example, chapter 14 of the *De Corpore et Sanguine Domini* by Paschasius Radbertus is replete with references to miracles that confirm the presence of the Body of the historical Christ in the host. Paschasius explicitly refers to the *vitae* and *exempla* of the saints to illustrate that the "mystical sacraments of the Body and Blood" could be seen in the form of a lamb or a child or with the color of flesh and blood. According to these accounts, a saint perceived a lamb once the host was broken or was able to identify the content of the chalice as pure blood. King Edward's vision of the Christ-child during the celebration of the Eucharist, as narrated in the Anglo-Norman *La Estoire de Seint Aedward le Rei* and magnificently illustrated in MS. Cambridge, University Library, Ee.3.59, fol. 21r, is another example of such a miraculous confirmation of the real presence.[48] In this way, what was hidden in mystery became clear in the miracle, even for the doubtful. Divine kindness thus fulfilled men's need to see the truth with their own eyes so that no one had to doubt the divine mysteries.[49]

In the school of Liège, reason does not immediately and entirely replace the miraculous. Alger's first theological source is most certainly not human reason. For him, reason is not sufficient to understand the divine mysteries,[50] whereas this is the

---

[47] See G. R. Evans, *The Thought of Gregory the Great*, Cambridge Studies in Medieval Life and Thought (Cambridge: Cambridge University Press, 1988), 41–54.
[48] The illumination is reproduced on the cover of this volume.
[49] See Paschasius Radbertus, *De corpore et sanguine Domini*, ed. Beda Paulus, CCCM 16 (Turnhout: Brepols, 1969), 85–92. The miracles included in this work were added by later editors and are not Paschasius's own. Two helpful articles on the question of miracles in the early scholastic period are Jessalyn Bird, "The Construction of Orthodoxy and the (De)construction of Heretical Attacks on the Eucharist in Pastoralia from Peter the Chanter's Circle in Paris," in *Texts and the Repression of Medieval Heresy*, ed. Caterina Bruschi and Peter Biller, York Studies in Medieval Theology 4 (York: York Medieval Press, 2003), 45–61, and Gary Macy, "Medieval Theology of the Eucharist and the Chapel of the Miracle Corporal," *Vivens homo* 18:1 (2007): 59–77.
[50] See Alger, *De sacramentis corporis et sanguinis Dominici*, PL 180: 740D1: "… quae ad hoc non suppetit …."

case for Berengar.[51] Berengar audaciously states that since the qualities of bread and wine remain the same after the consecration, since their color and smell do not change, the substance of bread and wine cannot have changed into the substance of the Body and Blood of Christ. For him, the use of miracles to explain the mystery of the Body and Blood of Christ is not reasonable; indeed, it offends God.[52] The master from Tours underlines this position by stating that reason is the image of God in man: *secundum rationem sit factus ad imaginem Dei*.[53]

Adelmann asserts that reason is unable to comprehend the inscrutable secrets of faith.[54] Alger, too, is well aware of the fact that many aspects of the faith seem contrary to reason, especially the mystery of the Body and Blood of the Lord.[55] Demonstrating this point, he emphasizes the importance of past authorities in his prologue to *De sacramentis*:

Quia ergo tot haereses, et si quae sunt aliae de sacramento corporis et sanguinis Christi pullulant, de veritate et virtute ipsius, aspirante divina gratia, quanto fidelius potero absolvam; non humana quidem ratione, quae ad hoc non suppetit, sed ipsius Christi sanctorumque testimoniis, quibus Ecclesia roborata consistit, a quibus quo firmius veram obtinet fidem, eo certius aeternam	Because there are so many known heresies—and possibly there exist even more—about the sacrament of the Body and Blood of Christ, I shall as faithfully as possible, and supported by divine grace, offer a solution regarding its reality and effect—not through human reason, which is insufficient for this, but supported by witnesses of Christ and His saints, through which the

---

[51] See Berengar, *Rescriptum* (see note 16 above), 85–6[1795–1803]: "Maximi plane cordis est per omnia ad dialecticam confugere, quia confugere ad eam ad rationem est confugere, quo qui non confugit, cum secundum rationem sit factus ad imaginem dei, suum honorem reliquit nec potest renovari de die in diem ad imaginem dei. Dialecticam beatus Augustinus tanta diffinitione dignatur, ut dicat: dialectica ars est artium, disciplina disciplinarum, novit discere, novit docere, scientes facere non solum vult, sed etiam facit." Berengar emphasizes the use of dialectics. If we say that Jesus is the cornerstone, this does not mean that we can carry him away: "Ubi ego scripsi: 'Sicut enim qui dicit: «Christus est summus angularis lapis», Christum non aufert, Christum esse omnino constituit, ita qui dicit: «panis altaris solummodo est sacramentum», vel: «panis altaris solummodo est corpus Christi», panem in altari esse non negat, panem et vinum esse confirmat in mensa dominica', verum, inquis tu, adnecteres, si ignarus veritatis priorem propositionis partem quisquam statueret, nisi forte figurato locutionis modo verbum illud proferret"(ibid., 68–9[1180–7]).

[52] See ibid., 82[1683–8]: "Per miraculum dicis ista fieri, admirationi deberi: verius dixisses ad iniuriam et contemptum dei vel, ut verba ponam beati Augustini, per flagitium vel facinus ista fieri, nec admirationi deberi, nisi ad contemptum admirationem accipias, secundum quod dicitur miratus Naaman quod iussus sit se immergere in Iordanem."

[53] Ibid., 85[1797–8].

[54] See Adelmann, "Letter from Adelmann to Berengar," pp. 72/74 below.

[55] See Alger, *De sacramentis*, PL 180:758[D8–11]: "… ratione videtur contrarium."

assequitur salutem. *Non enim*, ut ait Apostolus, *in persuasibilibus humanae sapientiae verbis, sed per stultitiam praedicationis placuit salvos facere credentes; quia, quod stultum est Dei, sapientius est hominibus; et quod infirmum est Dei, fortius est hominibus* (I Cor 1.21 & 2.4).[56]	Church can speak with authority. The firmer the true faith which one receives from them, the more certainly one gains eternal salvation. *Not, as the Apostle says, by persuasive words, but by the foolishness of our preaching, it pleased God to save those that believe. Because the foolishness of God is wiser than men; and the weakness of God is stronger than men.*

Recognizing the miraculous aspect of the Eucharist, Alger finds the conversion—the replacement of the substance of the bread by that of the Body—necessary to support not only the sacramental, but also the miraculous character of the Eucharist.[57] Like Ambrose, he asserts that God needs two extraordinary works to fulfill this mystery, one in the order of creation (He brings into existence things which were not before) and another in the order of alteration (He makes those things become what they were not).[58] Yet another miracle is necessary to prevent the sacrament from disintegrating during digestion or from being susceptible to any other kind of corruption.[59] God (Christ) uses this miracle so that the merits of the faithful may increase. For those who do not believe, they function as a sign for conversion.[60]

Unlike Alger, Adelmann offers no explanation for the conversion of bread and wine into the Body and Blood of Christ. The conversion happens invisibly and is a matter of faith. Repeating the teachings of the Church, he emphasizes the omnipotence of Christ. If He causes the change, we have to believe in it, since the Eucharist is the way in which He remains among us after the Ascension. Just like Alger, Adelmann adduces no miracles to prove his statements.[61]

---

[56] Ibid., PL 180:740^{C12-D9}.

[57] See ibid., 761^{B4-8}: "Facilius enim et certius creditur corpus Christi in illo sacramento fieri et esse, ubi corporaliter non fuerat, non solum pro sacramento, sed et pro miraculo, dum ibi panis desinit esse quod fuerat." On the miraculous character of the Eucharist, see also ibid., 758^{D8}–759^{A4}.

[58] See ibid., 767^{D9}–768^{A1}: "In quo notandum est quia B. Ambrosius ad comprobandum hujus mysterii tertium miraculum, duo mirabilia opera Dei praemisit; unum creationis, qua fecit existere quae non erant, alterum mutationis, qua ea quae erant fieri fecit quod non erant." Cf. Ambrose, *De mysteriis*, cap. 9, para. 52 (CSEL 73:112$^{41-3}$).

[59] See ibid., 810^{A8-B1}.

[60] See ibid., 819^{D11-14}.

[61] See Adelmann, "Letter from Adelmann to Berengar," p. 76 below.

(3) Authorities and Dialectics

The theologians of Liège must be situated in a long tradition that prefers authorities to dialectical reasoning. Moreover, they tend to choose very specific authorities; in fact, they quote almost no early medieval theologians, such as Gregory the Great, the Venerable Bede, and Alcuin. Instead, Alger and Adelmann rely primarily on the Bible, secondly on Augustine (or Pseudo-Augustine), and thirdly on certain classical authors (for example, Sallust, Virgil, Cicero, and Quintilian). Only as a last resort do they refer to medieval theologians.[62] Since, in matters of faith, a judgment based on sense perception must be distrusted, it is good to rely on the fame of authorities.[63] The use of authorities is accompanied by rhetorical questions: if Christ offers bread and wine as His Body and Blood, who could deny this? God created everything through His Word, and Christ changed water into wine at Canaan: why, then, should it not be possible for Him to change bread and wine into His Body and Blood?[64]

The use of authorities, including pseudonymous writings, combined with a lack of precise definitions and an inconsistent use of many theological concepts, can of course give rise to problems. For example, although Alger makes a distinction between *sacramentum* and *figura*, he confuses these concepts in the prologue to *De sacramentis*, where he writes: "Alii enim panem et vinum non mutatum, sed solum sacramentum, sicut aquam baptismatum, vel oleum chrismatis, corpus Christi non vere, sed figurate vocari dicunt ...."[65] Another problem has to do with a well-known decretal that Pope Innocent I (401–417) addressed to the bishop of Antioch, and in which he refused to accept Arian priests, because they considered baptism to be the

---

[62] A contemporary, Durandus of Troarn, quotes—in the same Eucharistic controversy—theologians such as Hincmar, Hilary of Poitiers, Amalarius of Metz, Paschasius Radbertus, and Fulbert of Chartres (besides the traditional authorities such as Augustine, Ambrose, and Gregory). Moreover, Durandus devotes the first pages of his *Liber de corpore et sanguine Christi* to the question concerning the use of authorities. Alger relies particularly heavily on Augustine, such that an abridgment of his *De sacramentis*, circulated under the title, *De sacramento altaris*, was frequently attributed to Augustine himself (see Georges Folliet, "Un abrégé du *De sacramento corporis et sanguinis Domini* d'Alger de Liège, mis sous le nom de S. Augustin," *Recherches augustiniennes* 8 [1972]: 261–99).

[63] See Adelmann, "Letter from Adelmann to Berengar," pp. 64/66 below: "Bonum est, frater, nobis parvulis sub istorum ducum titulis delitescere, quorum tam valida tam que probabilis est apud aecclesiasticas aures auctoritas, sanctarum virtutum fulgore et caelestis sapientiae luce prepollens, ut extremae iam sit dementiae vel de ratione fidei vel de ordine recte vivendi eis in aliquo refragari. Quare? Nonne homines erant et falli ab aliis atque ipsi fallere alios poterant? Ita enim dicit Scriptura verax, quia *omnis homo mendax*."

[64] See ibid., pp. 66/68 below.

[65] Alger, *De sacramentis*, PL 180:739D$^{4-7}$.

only spiritually profitable sacrament.[66] In Alger's theology, baptism always confers the sacramental *virtus* or *effectus* (that is, spiritual grace) even if it is administered by unworthy people or pagans. Therefore, it is always a *sacramentum ratum*, that is, it is spiritually profitable, provided only that it is conferred in the name of the Trinity upon a Catholic. The pope's decretal, however, appears to reject this theological position.[67] In the pope's opinion, there is no spiritual grace without the Holy Spirit so that such a baptism can never be *ratum*. Alger defends his own theological stance, explaining to his readers that statements made by the Church are relative and can vary. He spends a whole chapter on this question.[68] Nevertheless, in order to reconcile the papal decretal with his own opinion, Alger declares some sacraments administered by heretics to be *rata* and others *non rata*, although he stated earlier that none of the sacraments of the heretics were spiritually fruitful.[69] Perhaps this best reflects Alger's general opinion: sacraments administered outside the Church community can be valid, but are spiritually empty because they are not able to gain celestial grace for man: "vera quantum ad formam, inania tamen et falsa sunt quantum ad effectum."[70] The *forma* of the sacrament includes everything (even the imprinted character) except for its *virtus* (that is, spiritual grace).[71]

(4) Monastic Theology?

Alger has a characteristically monastic way of theologizing, apparent in the way he deals with authorities and in his method of arguing. On the one hand, he uses

---

[66] See Innocent I, *Epistola 24*, PL 20:550^{A6}: "solum baptisma ratum esse permittimus."

[67] See ibid., 550^{A8-10}: "… nec sanctum Spiritum eos habere ex illo baptismate illisque mysteriis arbitramur …."

[68] See Alger, *De misericordia et justitia*, cap. 24, PL 180:942^{C3-D10}/ Kretzschmar, *Alger von Lüttichs Traktat "De misericordia et iustitia"*, 332.

[69] Alger's early opinion, based on Jerome and the prophet Amos, appears in the following statement: "[N]ulla haereticorum sacramenta sint rata" (*De misericordia et justitia*, cap. 24, PL 180:940^{B8-9}/ Kretzschmar, *Alger von Lüttichs Traktat "De misericordia et iustitia,"* 328). His changed opinion reads as follows: "Quia ergo haereticis solum baptisma permittitur esse ratum et verum, quod tamen cum sit sine sanctificatione Spiritus, inutile et noxium; vitanda sunt revera omnia eorum sacramenta tam rata, quam non rata; quia, ut scriptum est: Omnia munda mundis, coinquinatis autem et infidelibus nihil mundum (Titus 1.15)" (ibid., 942^{D4-10}). This discussion must also be seen against the background of the eleventh-century debates about the validity of rituals performed by simoniacs. See Joseph H. Lynch, *Simoniacal Entry into Religious Life from 1000 to 1260: A Social, Economic, and Legal Study* (Columbus: Ohio State University Press, 1976).

[70] Alger, *De misericordia et justitia*, cap. 24, PL 180:951^{B14-16}/Kretzschmar, *Alger von Lüttichs Traktat "De misericordia et iustitia,"* 347.

[71] See Häring, "A Study in the Sacramentology of Alger (see note 38 above)," 47–8.

many quotations from authorities; on the other, he employs a method of "free association." He explains as follows why bread and wine are consecrated separately:

Ideo etiam corpus et sanguis divisim in sacramento videntur, ut quia Christus pro nobis mortuus est, nos qui corpore et anima perieramus, corpus per corpus, et animam per animam redimens, corpus et animam suam pro nostra redemptione in morte divisa fuisse signetur, dum corpus ejus in sepulcro jacuit, anima vero ad liberandas sanctorum animas ad inferna descendit.[72]	Therefore, the Body and Blood are even seen separately in the sacrament. In this manner, it may be indicated that the body and soul of Christ—having died for our redemption—are also separated in death. We die with body and soul, and He has redeemed our body by His body and our soul by His soul. While His body lay in the grave, His soul truly descended into hell to liberate the souls of the saints.

Alger never criticizes quotations from authorities and Scripture. Only occasionally does he develop or explain an argument made by his authorities. To prove the presence of the Body and Blood of Christ in the Eucharist, he endlessly repeats Augustine's comment on the promise of the Eucharist in the Gospel of John 6:54: "Those who eat my flesh and drink my blood, have eternal life, and I will raise them up on the last day."[73] Exactly the same is true for Adelmann, who explicitly says that he wishes to walk on the safe paths trodden by the Fathers.[74] Since the truth of the

---

[72] Alger, *De sacramentis*, PL 180:826[C7–14]. Another good example of his way of reasoning can be found in chapter 4 of the second book of *De sacramentis*, where he answers the question as to why faith is necessary for the sacrament of the Body of Christ. He explains that, without faith, the sacrament cannot be understood and, without faith, we cannot be saved. He uses Genesis to illustrate this point: "Quia videlicet falsa fide mundus periit, quando Adam plus diabolo quam Deo credere praesumpsit, dum in ligno scientiae boni et mali vetito plus speravit divinitatem assequi, quae ab hoste promittebatur, quam incurrere mortem quam Deus minabatur. Sicut ergo diabolus non umbram in ligno inobedientiae, sed ipsum verum et visibilem fructum exhibens, promisit id quod non videbatur, scilicet, eritis sicut dii (Gen. 3, 5), sic et Deus non umbram, sed ipsum qui in ligno pependit obedientiae, in suo visibili sacramento exhibens, promittit vitam aeternam quae non videtur, ut dum ea re plus ei modo creditur quam hosti, ut dignum est, sanetur hac vera fide illa perfida fides, qua olim plus diabolo quam sibi injuste creditum est. Sicut igitur non in ligno vetito, sic nec in Christi sacramento debet visus aut gustus, sed fidei vigere judicium, quia sicut pomum visu decorum et suave ad comedendum, cibus vitalis videbatur, et mortem intulit, sic e contrario sacramentum corporis et sanguinis Christi videtur cibus mortalitatis nostrae, cum vere vita aeterna sit."
[73] See ibid., 772[C], 774[C], 775[B–D], 776[C–D]: "Dixit ergo eis Iesus: Amen, amen dico vobis: Nisi manducaveritis carnem Filii hominis, et biberitis eius sanguinem, non habebitis vitam in vobis."
[74] See Adelmann, "Letter from Adelmann to Berengar," p. 62 below: "Nos enim sanctiorem vitam salubriorem que doctrinam catholici et christianissimi viri una experti sumus, et nunc eius apud deum precibus adiuvari sperare debemus: neque enim putandus est memoriam, in qua nos tanquam in sinu materno semper ferebat, amisisse, aut vero caritas Christi, qua sicut filios amplectebatur, in eo extincta est, sed absque dubio memor nostri et diligens plenius, quam cum in corpore mortis huius

Eucharist is universally believed, it is impossible that it could be erroneous.[75] Divine veracity guarantees the truth of both Scripture and the authorities.

With this stance, Alger is a typical monastic thinker. This becomes particularly clear in chapter 17 of *De sacramentis*, where Alger states that the Body of Christ is signified in two or three ways. According to Alger, there is no difference between Jerome, who says that the Body and Blood of Christ must be understood in a double way (*quantum ad duplicem ejusdem substantiae formam*), and Augustine, who considers the Church to be a third way, namely, the mystical Body of Christ.[76] "Hac de causa etiam sancti de corpore et sanguine Domini varie loquuntur," explains Alger, "sed non contrarie …."[77] Confusion arises only when one mixes up (*transferre et convertere*) the different forms of Christ's Body *in sacramento*, *in humana forma*, and *in ecclesia*.[78]

For the theologians of Liège the latter seems to be a crucial distinction. Since they do not explicitly differentiate between substance and accidents, they explain the nature of the conversion in terms of the different bodies of Christ.[79] These theologians distinguish first the historical Body of Christ, which was born of the Virgin Mary, died on the Cross, and sits at the right hand of the Father. Secondly, they mention Christ's Body that is present in the Eucharist, and thirdly there is the Body constituted by the Church community. The lines between the different bodies ought not to be drawn too strictly, since in the Eucharist the two other bodies are also present: it is a commemorative meal, so that the historical Body is present, and it is a community meal which anticipates the union of the faithful with their Lord. The substance of Christ's Body always remains the same.

---

peregrinaretur, invitat ad se votis et taciti precibus, obtestans per secreta illa et vespertina colloquia, quae nobis cum in hortulo iuxta capellam de civitate illa, quam deo volente senator nunc possidet, sepius habebat, et obsecrans per lacrimas, quas, interdum in medio sermone prorumpens, exundante sancti ardoris impetu emanabat, ut illuc omni studio properemus, viam regiam directim gradientes, sanctorum patrum vestigiis observantissime inherentes, ut nullum prorsus [in] diverticulum, nullam in novam et fallacem semitam desiliamus, ne forte in laqueos et scandala incidamus, quia, sicut ait psalmista, *iuxta iter scandalum posuerunt mihi*."

[75] Alger must have borrowed this argument of Lanfranc, because he knew the *Liber de corpore et sanguini Domini*, where Lanfranc writes: "Interroga universos qui Latinae linguae nostrarumve litterarum notitiam perceperunt. Interroga Graecos, Armenos, seu cujuslibet nationis quoscunque Christianos homines; uno ore hanc fidem se testantur habere. Porro si universalis Ecclesiae fides falsa existit, aut nunquam fuit Catholica Ecclesia, aut periit" (PL 150:441[A4–10]). Alger elaborates on this argument in *De sacramentis corporis et sanguinis Dominici* (PL 180:780[A15–B3]): "Cum enim omnes gentes ita se credere glorientur, si salutis benedictione carent, utrobique veritas Dei et in prophetia et in Evangelio periclitatur."

[76] See Alger, *De sacramentis*, PL 180:790[C6–D11].

[77] Ibid., 790[C1–2].

[78] Ibid., 790[D11–13].

[79] See Adelmann, "Letter from Adelmann to Berengar," p. 78 below: "multiplex est corpus Christi," and p. 84 below: "de tripartita corporis Christi distinctio."

Unlike Berengar, who deals differently—more dialectically—with this problem, Alger believes that faith suffices.[80] He is convinced that Christ speaks to us through the Scriptures, because Christ is the truth and the way.[81] One scriptural argument legitimizes another.

Ut enim ait Augustinus contra Felicianum: "Si incomprehensibilis est ratio, et veritas prompta est, facilius in negotiis fidei testimoniis creditur, quam ratio investigatur." Hae igitur Scripturae quamvis cum propheticis et apostolicis aequam auctoritatis excellentiam non obtineant, eamdem tamen fidem cum fidelibus et sanctis antecessoribus nostris nos tenere sufficienter probant, hujusque probationis in hoc sibi perfectam auctoritatem vindicant, quia nisi ita esset ut docent, in sacris canonibus vel Romanorum pontificum decretis, sicut haeretica vel apocrypha scripta damnatae essent, nec eas in Ecclesia Catholici viri vel legerent vel recitarent. Cum ergo praeteriti et praesentes fideles ubique terrarum hoc credant et hoc astruant, si haec universalis Ecclesiae fides vera ad salutem non exstitit, aut nunquam Catholica Ecclesia fuit, aut periit. Sed aut non fuisse, aut periisse Ecclesiam nemo Catholicus consenserit.[82]	As Augustine asserts against Felician: "If reason is incomprehensible and truth is manifest, then in discussions testimonies of faith are more easily believed than reason is investigated." So, those Scriptures, although they do not rise to the same excellence of authority as the prophets and apostles, sufficiently prove that we uphold the same faith with our faithful and saintly predecessors; if it was not this which they taught, they would have been condemned as heretical or apocryphal writings in sacred canons or in decrees of the Roman pontiffs, and Catholic men in the Church should not read or recite them. Thus, since all past and present faithful all over the world believe this and build on it, if this belief of the universal Church did not truly exist for salvation, it either never was the Catholic Church, or it perished. But that the Church either never was, or perished, no Catholic would accept.

On the whole, Alger is satisfied with the miraculous character of the Eucharist.[83] He does not need a dialectical understanding of this mystery. It is simply another miracle of the God who made a virgin conceive.

Occasionally Alger makes use of other methods of reasoning to confirm his authorities, although these are not dialectical in the strict sense. One of his rational

---

[80] See Alger, *De sacramentis*, PL 180:742[D13]–743[A7]: "Ut, sicut illa quae incomprehensibilia sunt sensibus non minus esse creduntur, sic quae sunt incomprehensibilia intellectibus humanis non minus esse credantur. Ut igitur ait Apostolus, Deum nunc per speculum et in aenigmate (I Cor. 13.12) contemplantes, multum de ipso cognoscimus, si ipsum nobis incomprehensibilem, in his quae ex nihilo fecit, mirabilem in seipso credamus mirabiliorem."

[81] See ibid., 776[B9–11]: "… ut Pater de coelo jussit, audiamus; et quia veritas et vita est, veracem esse sicut vere est, credamus." Cf. ibid., 794[B13–C5].

[82] Ibid., PL 180:779[D6]–780[A10].

[83] See ibid., 810[A2–8]: "Ad quod respondendum est, quod sicut Deus in omnibus est mirabilis, sic et in istis. Facit enim in suo sacramento accidentales qualitates existere per se, quod in caeteris est impossibile. Sed qui virgini dedit fecunditatem sine semine, quid mirum si sine substantiae fundamento facit qualitates existere?"

arguments is intended to give an answer to one of the most difficult questions in the controversy on the Eucharist, namely, the question regarding the conversion of the substances of bread and wine into the true Body and Blood of Christ while the qualities attached to these substances remain unchanged: "Quod remanentibus qualitatibus suis substantia panis et vini in verum corpus Christi mutetur." Chapter 7 of the first Book of *De sacramentis* is devoted to this theological crux. A monastic answer like that of his contemporary Guitmond of Aversa (in *De corporis et sanguinis Domini veritate*, written around 1073–1078) was based on the Scriptures: during the Transfiguration, Christ's face shone like the sun and his garments became as white as light, and after the Resurrection, Christ showed Himself to Mary Magdalene as a gardener, and to the disciples at Emmaus as a pilgrim.[84] In other words, Christ appears in a variety of guises to his disciples. Alger tries a more rational argument. It would be truly contrary to reason, he maintains, if the bread of the Eucharist changed totally into the Body of Christ, as if it no longer resembled bread at all. This would be fantastic. But fantasy and illusion are contrary to the nature of Scripture.[85]

Furthermore, it is evident to reason that the bread must look like bread after the consecration, since if nothing remained of the species of the changed bread, the merits of faith would diminish.[86] Faith is needed in order to recognize the miracle, since in the consecration of the sacrament the bread itself vanishes altogether. Of course, the old argument that it would be horrible to eat from a body that looked like a corpse remains valid. For the benefit of perception, the sensible species of bread and wine remain intact.[87] After this argumentation, he continues in the expected way: "We have seen how much this is not only contrary to reason, but also to the authorities."[88] Adelmann for his part only stresses the importance of faith and quotes the Apostle, "for we walk by faith, not by sight" (2 Cor. 5:7) and, "Faith is the assurance of things hoped for, proof of things not seen" (Heb. 11:1).[89]

In scholastic theology, we find no new answers to the question of why Body and Blood appear as the species of bread and wine. Peter Lombard repeats all the

---

[84] See Guitmond of Aversa, *De corporis et sanguinis Christi veritate in eucharistia*, PL 149:1481^{C13-D7}: "De colore quoque et caeteris hujusmodi accidentibus non est difficilis ratio, cum ipse Dominus se per diversas legatur species discipulis demonstrasse, et nunc eis solitum colorem ostendisse, nunc ad instar solis et nivis trasfiguratum resplenduisse (Matth. XVII), nunc se exhibuisse tanquam peregrinum (Luc. XXIV), nunc apparuisse velut hortulanum (Joan. XX), aliquando speciem exhibuisse ministrantis, aliquando formam tenuisse docentis."
[85] See Alger, *De sacramentis*, PL 180:758^{D8}–759^{A4} and 759^{C6-18}.
[86] I would like to put another question to Alger in this context: If faith is the fruit of divine grace, what merits can it have at all?
[87] See ibid., 759^{C1-3}.
[88] Ibid., 759^{D7-8}: "[Q]uomodo id non solum rationi, sed et auctoritati sit contrarium, videamus." He then continues quoting Augustine and explains why Berengar's opinion is heretical.
[89] See Adelmann, "Letter from Adelmann to Berengar," p. 70 below.

arguments that can already be discovered in Alger's treatise. Firstly, "ut fides haberet meritum"; in other words, faith, of which human reason explores the meaning, would have no merit if the Body and Blood appeared as such in the Eucharist. Secondly, Peter Lombard offers the traditional argument of Pope Gregory the Great: "Ne abhorreret animus quod cerneret oculus." Men are not in the habit of eating raw flesh and drinking blood.[90] We can say, then, that the Liège theologians' use of rational argumentation already points toward scholasticism, so that it is not true that monastic theology is somehow irrational.

Even more than his rational way of arguing, Alger's attempts to systematize and to define the theological concepts that were to become highly important in the following century, begin to resemble scholasticism. Take, for example, the distinction, already discussed, between *sacramentum*, *res sacramenti*, and *effectus sacramenti*. He also uses logical deductions in some of his argumentations where he does not invoke authorities. An example is his attempt to counter the Berengarians in chapter 8 of *De sacramentis*.[91] In this context, he has to refute the so-called *impanatores*, who tried to resolve the question of the conversion of bread and wine into Body and Blood in a peculiar way. Like Lanfranc, Berengar denied any substantial conversion, but he failed to address all the consequences of his position. The generation following him did so, and thoroughly. These *impanatores* accepted the substantial presence of the Body of Christ in the Eucharist, but they explained it in a way that had to be considered heretical: the Body of the Lord is truly present, but hidden in the bread—it is "impanated."[92] This is a kind of middle position. The *impanatores* safeguard the true presence of Christ in the Eucharist, and at the same time they can maintain that the substance of bread and wine do not change. To prove the *impanatio*, they use an ingenious analogy: bread and wine become the Body and Blood of Christ, just as the Word became flesh.

To counter this argumentation, Alger asserts that the Eucharistic bread truly hides the divinity of Christ, just as Christ's divinity was hidden by his humanity; however, this does not imply a personal union of the bread and Christ, in which the substance of each is guaranteed. He solves this question primarily by using authorities, but also

---

[90] Peter Lombard, *Sententiae in IV libris distinctae* (see note 25 above) IV, dist. 11, cap. 3 (2:299).
[91] Alger once uses the term *dialectici* to designate those who argue by means of dialectics (*De sacramentis*, PL 180:809^{D8}). There seems to be little evidence that Berengar had any followers in his teachings on the Eucharist. See Gary Macy, "Berengar's Legacy as Heresiarch," in *Auctoritas und Ratio: Studien zu Berengar von Tours*, ed. Peter Ganz, Robert Burchard Constantijn Huygens, and Friedrich Niewöhner, Wolfenbütteler Mittelalter-Studien 2 (Wiesbaden: Harrassowitz, 1990), 47–67.
[92] Alger defines the position of the *impanatores* as follows: "Quamvis autem sacramentum superius a re sacramenti, tanquam figura a veritate, satis distinctum sit, errantes tamen quidam de quibusdam sanctorum verbis, dicunt ita personaliter in pane impanatum Christum, sicut in carne humana personaliter incarnatum Deum" (*De sacramentis*, PL 180:754$^{A15–B5}$).

by a nice example of dialectical reasoning. The utterance *Verbum fit caro* is of another order than *panis fit caro*. The Word became flesh by being born out of flesh, not by changing Himself into flesh, thus becoming what He was not before. The bread, on the contrary, becomes the flesh of Christ; it does become something that it was not before.[93] Alger reaches his conclusion *admirabiliter* (said Father Maurice de la Taille in his famous work on the Mass),[94] preparing Thomas Aquinas's teachings on the transubstantiation:[95]

Sed longe aliter panis et vinum fit caro et sanguis Christi in sacramento per gratiam, quam in cujuslibet vel etiam ipsius Christi stomacho per naturam. In stomacho enim Christi panis et vinum, non mutata vel deficiente substantia, sed forma, novam carnem et novum sanguinem, corruptioni aliquatenus obnoxium, sicut in caeteris hominibus generavit; in sacramento autem, mutata substantia non forma, panis et vinum non fit nova caro et novus sanguis, sed existens substantia panis et vini mutatur in coexistentem substantiam corporis Christi; ita ut novitate sua nihil in ipso innovet, mutatione sua nihil immutet.[96]	Totally different are the way in which bread and wine become the Body and Blood of Christ through grace in the sacrament, and the way in which they become it in the stomach of Christ through nature. Indeed, in Christ's stomach, bread and wine—whose substances are not changed or destroyed, but whose appearances are changed—have produced, as in any other man, a new body and new blood that are to a degree subject to corruption. In the sacrament, however, after the substance but not the appearance has changed, bread and wine do not become new flesh or new blood. Instead, the existing substance of bread and wine is changed into the coexisting substance of the Body of Christ, in such a way that there is nothing new in Christ through this newness, and nothing is changed in Christ through this conversion.

Alger anticipates scholastic theology (and the dogma of transubstantiation) by emphasizing the fact that the conversion of bread and wine into the Body and

---

[93] See ibid., 755[A15–B6]: "Verbum fit caro, et nascitur caro de carne, assumendo carnem, non mutatum in carnem: sic factum quod non fuerat, ut non desisteret esse quod erat. Panis autem fit eadem caro, non nascitur caro, nec assumit carnem, sed mutatur in carnem; sic factus quod non erat, ut desistat esse quod fuerat." And, a little further: "Non enim ita sumere dicendus est in altari speciem vel formam panis, sicut in utero virginali speciem vel formam carnis: cum in utero sumpserit speciem vel formam cum substantia, in altari vero speciem vel formam panis mutata et non permanente substantia" (ibid., 755[C13–D3]).
[94] Mauritius de la Taille, *Mysterium fidei, de augustissimo corporis et sanguinis Christi sacrificio atque sacramento. Elucidationes L in tres libros distinctae* (Paris: Beauchesne, 1924), p. 637, col. 1.
[95] See Gary Macy, "The Dogma of Transubstantiation in the Middle Ages," *Journal of Ecclesiastical History* 45 (1994): 11–41.
[96] Alger, *De sacramentis*, PL 180:766[C1–13].

Blood of Christ must be considered as affecting the transformed material species exclusively, while the Body of Christ itself does not change:

Super omnia enim est mirabile existentem substantiam panis, in coexistentem substantiam carnis suae convertere; quod est non videri, quod videtur non esse; ipsamque carnem, cum sit localis, praesentem in coelo et in terra vere et substantialiter esse; et cum vere caro comesta, et sanguis ejus bibitus fuerit a populo, ipsum tamen Christum vivum et integrum suo permanere in regno.[97]	Indeed, wonderful above all is the conversion of the existing substance of bread into the coexisting substance of His flesh. This cannot be seen, nor does it appear to be so; and yet the same flesh, because it is located, is truly and substantially present in heaven and on earth. Nevertheless, when the flesh is truly eaten and the blood truly drunk by the people, the living and untouched Christ Himself remains in His kingdom.

Like Alger, Adelmann does not fight Berengar on his own terms: he makes a clear distinction between Berengar's dialectics and his own, more traditional theological hermeneutics.[98] Adelmann discriminates between three cognitive functions: a merely sensible, a sensible-spiritual, and a purely spiritual.[99] Apart from these functions, Adelmann recognizes yet another function with which we can perceive God without mediation. This is not a natural power, but a gift of grace: faith.[100] His conclusion is simple (and very unsatisfactory to Berengar): to know the essence of sacraments, our natural epistemological tools are inadequate. We need faith.[101] Take baptism, for instance: our senses can perceive only the water, so that we need faith to see what really happens "inside" the sacrament.[102] Ultimately, Christ guarantees the truth of the sacrament.[103]

---

[97] Ibid., 741A10–B1.
[98] For a summary of Adelmann's views regarding the sacraments, see Geiselmann, *Die Eucharistielehre der Vorscholastik* (note 5 above), 303–05.
[99] See Adelmann, "Letter from Adelmann to Berengar," p. 72 below.
[100] See ibid., p. 74: "Hic prorsus evigila atque animadverte, preter sensum et rationem tercium quiddam prestantius, quo deum ipsum attingere possumus, nos habere, non innatum sed ex gratia dei conlatum, hoc vero esse fidem christianam."
[101] See ibid., p. 72: "Conamur enim adiuvante divina gratia ostendere quod nulla humana facultas, quae plane et ipsa est divina largitas, nequaquam tamen sufficiens sit, quamlibet se extendat, ad comprehendandam altitudinem sacramentorum, quibus initiamur et perficimur ad aeternam salutem quae est in Christo Iesu domino nostro." Also see ibid., p. 70: "Ut ergo fides exerceatur credendo quod non apparet, vitale sacramentum sub specie corporea, ut anima in corpore, utiliter latet."
[102] See ibid., p. 74: "Nam cum in baptismo nihil amplius quam aquam sensus et ratio deprehendat, fides introrsum descendens virtutem in eo vivificam perspicue atque simpliciter intuetur."
[103] See ibid., p. 66: "Quis hoc ita esse non credit, nisi qui aut Christo non credit aut ipsum hoc dixisse non credit?"

Unfortunately, Alger's theology is not free of inconsistencies. The first excerpt[104] provides an important example of such an inconsistency. As Alger writes, "One has to distinguish sacrament and mystery, because the former is a sign signifying something visible, while a mystery signifies something hidden. Occasionally the one is taken for the other, as we said above. You accept your mystery as if it is a concealing and concealed mystery, and a sacrament as if it is a signifying and signified sacrament." A sacrament signifies something; a mystery is something hidden signified by a sign. But a sacrament also reveals something hidden. However, the problem becomes even more complex. The excerpt speaks of a *mysterium occultans et occultum* and a *sacramentum signans et signatum*. According to Alger, this may cause wonder, because it is amazing that a sacrament should simultaneously play the roles of *sacramentum* and *res sacramenti*, in other words, that it can be taken *pro signo* (*sacramentum*) and *pro signato* (*corpus Christi*).[105] His main argument is a dictum attributed to Augustine: *Corpus Christi et veritas et figura est*.[106] Berengar is much clearer on this matter: the *sacramenta* (bread and wine) are *figurae* and *similitudines* of what they signify, whereas the *res sacramentorum* (Body and Blood) are not *signa* of anything else. Berengar reproaches Adelmann for confusing *res* and *signa*, but—if he had lived long enough—he could have accused Alger of the same confusion.[107]

The distinction between sacrament and mystery is not the only inconsistency in Alger's work.[108] The title of the treatise presents a similar problem. Although Alger speaks of the sacraments or the twofold sacrament of the Body and Blood of Christ[109]

---

[104] Quoted on p. 8 above.
[105] See Alger, *De sacramentis*, PL 180:752A6–8. Häring notes (in "A Study in the Sacramentology of Alger" [see note 38 above], 57): "The reason why the word was found with these two different meanings was Lanfranc's refusal to accept Berengar's clear distinction between the visible *sacramentum* and the invisible *res*."
[106] Alger, *De sacramentis*, PL 180:752^{A9-10}. The author of this sentence is, in fact, Paschasius Radbertus, *De coprore et sanguine Domini* (see note 48 above), 29$^{43-6}$: "Sed si ueraciter inspicimus, iure simul ueritas et figura dicitur, ut sit figura uel caracter ueritatis quod exterius sentitur, ueritas uero quicquid de hoc mysterio interius recte intelligitur aut creditur." Abelard also quotes this sentence, but he makes a clear distinction between *veritas* and *figura*: "Corpus Christi et veritas et figura est. Veritas, dum corpus Christi et sanguis virtute spiritus in verbo ipsius ex panis vini que substantia efficitur. Figura vero, quod exterius sentitur" (Peter Abelard, *Sic et non*, ed. Blanche B. Boyer and Richard McKeon [Chicago: University of Chicago Press, 1976–1977], 399$^{605-08}$).
[107] See Berengar, "Letter from Berengar to Adelmann," p. 94 below.
[108] Another example: Alger stresses the division between the visible *sacramentun* and the invisible *res*, but then says that the true Body of Christ (invisible after the Resurrection) is the *sacramentum* of the visible Body. This case is discussed in Häring, "A Study in the Sacramentology of Alger" (note 38 above), 57–8.
[109] See Alger, *De sacramentis*, PL 180:826^{B10-13}: "Dicuntur autem duo diversa sacramenta panis et vinum, quantum ad diversas suas species, cum tamen sint unum, quantum ad unam eamdem suam significationem."

and not of the one sacrament of the Body and Blood of Christ, he also explicitly mentions that the two visible species (*sacramenta*) are one, because they have one and the same signification, even if they are consecrated separately (*cum utrumque unus sit Christus immortalis, indivisus*).[110] Further elaboration of this statement is lacking.

(5) Conclusion

In his *Eulogy for the Scholar Alger*, Alger's biographer Nicholas of Liège gives an accurate description of Alger's significance, a description that applies to the school of Liège in general: He was Catholic concerning doctrine (*quam doctrina Catholicus*) and wrote useful books for the Catholic faith (*Catholicae Fidei certe valde utiles*), in which nothing could be found that was opposed to the teachings of the saints or to the Catholic faith (*in quo nihil invenitur Sanctorum dictis dissonum, nihil Catholicae Fidei contrarium*).[111] The theologians of Liège do not only echo Carolingian controversies (such as discussions regarding the Church and sacramentology), but they also fall back on Carolingian methodology, according to which quoting authorities is more important than the logical consistency of the argumentation. Thus, Nicholas provides an accurate description in depicting an important member of this school as somewhat traditional.

The school of Liège does not break with traditional teachings, but applies them to contemporary developments. Major insights of the Liégeois theologians are the distinction between *sacramentum*, *res sacramenti*, and *effectus sacramenti* (in this phase the distinction is only applied to the Eucharist) and the attempt to formulate general principles (for instance, the importance of intent in the administration of the sacraments, the importance of the invocation of the divine name to make sacraments valid, and the rule, *omnia sacramenta suae gratiae esse deputentur*).[112] The idea which states that it must be Christ Himself who administers the sacraments is extended to the Eucharist. Not all these developments are brand new, but the theologians of Liège summarize the then current developments in generally accepted terms (not yet apodictic statements) in order to forestall many wearing questions and exhausting quarrels. This is certainly true of Alger. Adelmann is still very

---

[110] Ibid., 826^{B3-4}. In the first excerpt cited in this chapter we noticed a similar case: *caro* can mean "flesh" as well as "soul," but *anima* can mean "flesh" as well as "soul" also.

[111] Jean Mabillon, *Vetera analecta, sive collectio veterum aliquot operum & opusculorum omnis generis, carminum, epistolarum, diplomatum epitaphiorum, &c.* (Paris: Montalant, 1723), 129–30, quoted in Häring, "A Study in the Sacramentology of Alger," 41. The last phrase is meant as a statement specifically on Alger's work concerning the sacraments.

[112] Alger, *De sacramentis*, PL 180:852^{B13-14}.

involved in the Berengarian controversy, whereas Alger—a generation later—can keep some distance from it.

In brief, Alger and Adelmann contributed to the further medieval development of the Augustinian definition of the sacraments. Whereas Augustine's concise definition (*sacramentum, id est sacrum signum*) stated that a sacrament was a *signum*, the Liège theologians followed Isidore: a sacrament was both *signum* and *signatum*. In Peter Lombard's *Sentences*, this intuition became part of a full-fledged theory. At the same time, the theologians of Liège introduced the notion of intentionality (not a prerogative of Abelard alone!) during a period when canonists placed emphasis on the external aspects of the sacraments and the juridical conditions to validate them. There is another reason why Adelmann and Alger can be considered pre-scholastic: they were inclined to define their theological concepts ever more precisely. Very occasionally they reasoned dialectically, but in general their hermeneutics was based on authorities. This is why they may be called conservative. Contrary to Berengar, they stood in a tradition in which the concept of sacrament slowly evolved in the direction of its scholastic and Tridentine definitions.

Adelmann of Liège's Life

Reconstructing Adelmann's life is made difficult by the lack of source material.[1] Adelmann of Liège—in Latin, Adelmannus or Almannus Leodiensis[2]—was born around the year 1000 in the diocese of Liège.[3] The precise location and date of his birth remain unknown. He was still young when Bishop Reginard made him a subdeacon and allowed him to continue his education at the renowned school of Chartres from 1025 to 1028 under the illustrious Fulbert of Chartres (ca. 960–1028).[4] Berengar of Tours (ca. 1000–1088) was one of his schoolmates at Chartres, but Adelmann was slightly the older of the two.

Upon his return to Liège he wrote the first version of a song (or poem) that was posthumously entitled *Rhythmus alphabeticus de viris illustribus*. The song is primarily an ode to his celebrated schoolmaster Fulbert, but also to many other masters, scholars and Church officials. The song probably dates from somewhere between 1028 (after Fulbert's death) and 1033. That *terminus ad quem* is based on a sentence that only appears in the first version of the song: "Omnes uno funerati dormiunt quinquennio."[5] Every person he mentioned had died in the lustrum following

---

[1] Numerous historical testimonies on the life and thought of Adelmann are collected in "De veritate corporis et sanguinis Domini in Eucharistia, ad Berengarium epistola," in *Veterum Brixiae episcoporum S. Philastrii et S. Gaudentii opera, nec non B. Ramperti, & Vener. Adelmanni opuscula*, ed. Paulus Galeardus (Brixen: ex typographia Joannis Mariae Rizzardi, 1738), 413–22, at 409–12, and in *Adelmanni Brixiae episcopi de veritate corporis et sanguinis domini ad Berengarium epistola, nunc primum e codice Guelpherbytano emendata et vltra tertiam partem suppleta, cum epistola Berengarii ad Adelmannum et variis scriptis ad Adelmannum pertinentibus*, ed. Conrad Arnold Schmidt (Brunswick: Typis officinae librariae orphanotrophei, 1770), 50–62 and 63–79. Biographical data can also be found in Angelo Calogera, "De Adelmanni Brixiani episcopi emortuali anno atque vindiciis N.N. sacerdotis Brixiani ad concivem suum epistola," *Raccolta d'opuscoli scientifici e filologici* 47 (1752): i–xvi.

[2] Sigebert of Gembloux calls him "Almannus," but he calls himself "Adelmannus" both in his letter to Berengar and in the two versions of his poem.

[3] On his Walloon heritage: Hubert Silvestre, "Quelle était la langue maternelle d'Adelman de Liège, évêque de Brescia (†1061)," *La vie wallonne* 36 (1962): 43–9. On the year of his birth around 1005, see idem, "Notice sur Adelman de Liège, évêque de Brescia (†1061)," *Revue d'histoire ecclésiastique* 56 (1961): 855–71, esp. 859 n. 3.

[4] See Loren C. MacKinney, *Bishop Fulbert and Education at the School of Chartres*, Texts and Studies in the History of Medieval Education 4 (Notre Dame, Ind.: Medieval Institute, 1957), and Jules Alexandre Clerval, *Les écoles de Chartres au moyen âge du Ve au XVIe siècle* (Paris: Picard, 1895; reprinted, Geneva: Slatkine, 1977), esp. 34–5, 40, and 50–140.

[5] See p. 114 below in this volume.

Fulbert's death.[6] Later, when he was writing his famous letter to Berengar, he also prepared a new version of the song. It is not known, however, if the song belongs to this letter, or to another letter now lost.[7]

Around 1030–1031 Adelmann became master at the cathedral of Saint Lambert in Liège. He succeeded Wazo (ca. 985–1048), who had become bishop of Liège. After Adelmann, another eminent representative of the school of Liège, Gozechinus (ca. 1000–1080),[8] would fill the same position. The names of several of Adelmann's students are known, such as William, who later became abbot of Saint-Arnoul in Metz, and Lambert, a monk at Saint-Laurence in Liège and the author of a *Vita Heriberti*. The three verses Adelmann dedicated to Lambert were probably written during his period as master at the cathedral:

Vive puer, magni spes auspiciumque poete!	Live well, beloved son, the hope on higher
Pieriis cordi iam sunt tua scripta puellis;	poetry! Your word already sounds in the
Ante mihi gratus, posthac gratissimus esto.[9]	hearts of the Muses. You are beloved to me, be it, from now on, even more.

Around 1044 his tenure as master ended, this being the year when he was succeeded by Gozechinus. It was probably not long afterwards that he moved to Speyer. It is unclear what his duties in that city entailed. Was he a master there, too? After having stayed in that town for several years, he wrote his famous letter to Berengar (possibly around 1049).[10] Adelmann had been aware of Berengar's heterodox views for some time. He also addressed a letter, now lost, to a certain Paulinus, *primicerius* of Metz, asking him to verify whether the heretical opinions of which he had heard were indeed being proclaimed by Berengar.

---

[6] See Silvestre, "Notice sur Adelman de Liège," 859 n. 8. Balau believes the first version dates from before 1031; see Sylvain Balau, *Les sources de l'histoire de Liège au moyen âge. Étude critique* (Brussels: H. Lamertin, 1903), esp. 161.

[7] See Julien Havet, "Poème rythmique d'Adelman de Liège," *Notices et documents publiés par la Société de l'histoire de France à l'occasion du 50ᵉ anniversaire de sa fondation* (Paris: Renouard, 1884), 71–92, esp. 75.

[8] See Gozechinus, "Gozechini epistola ad Walcherum," in *Apologiae duae*, ed. R. B. C. Huygens, CCCM 62 (Turnhout: Brepols, 1985), 1–43.

[9] MS. London, British Library, Add. 26788, fol. 90r, transcribed in Karl Hampe, "Reise nach England vom Juli 1895 bis Februar 1896, II.," *Neues Archiv der Gesellschaft für ältere deutsche Geschichtskunde zur Beförderung einer Gesammtausgabe der Quellenschriften deutscher Geschichten des Mittelalters* 22 (1897): 335–415, at 376. The title of the poem in this manuscript is *Adelmannus episcopus ad eundem adhuc puerum*.

[10] See Silvestre, "Notice sur Adelman de Liège," 861. Havet dates the letter 1052 or 1053 (Havet, "Poème rythmique," 75), but Silvestre follows Balau, *Les sources de l'histoire de Liège*, 158 n. 7.

Adelmann fruitlessly waited for an answer for two years before deciding to follow up with a long letter to Berengar which is rather like a small treatise on the Eucharist. He tried to persuade his old fellow student to disavow his heterodox views and return to the right way. Berengar's answer to the letter has been preserved and contains, *in nucleo*, the doctrine that he was later to develop in more detail in his correspondence with Lanfranc.[11] During his stay in Speyer, Adelmann also wrote, besides the letter to Berengar, a second version of his *Rhythmus* (which he also sent to Berengar) and a letter to Hermann II, the archbishop of Cologne (1036–1056).[12] These letters are the last known documents by Adelmann's hand, although in the past, several more were attributed to him.[13]

It is possible that Adelmann stayed in Speyer for fifteen years, perhaps as *magister*, but there is no certain proof to support this.[14] It is conjectured that he left there at the start of 1059, since he became bishop of the Italian city of Brescia (Lombardy) some time before the month of April of that year. Two years later, on April 10, 1061, he died there under tumultuous circumstances. It seems that he took part in a synod in Rome in April, 1060, where an anathema was pronounced against Simonians and Nicolaitans. Upon returning to his own diocese, he turned out to be the only Lombardian bishop to promulgate these strict decrees. His own priests rebelled against him, endangering his life. Perhaps their ill treatment was the direct cause of his death one year after the synod.[15] He was interred in the small church of SS. Faustino e Giovitta. In 1612 his remains, together with those of three of his predecessors, were moved to a "more noble spot" that has remained unknown to the present day.[16]

Hubert Silvestre, a former professor at the Université Lovanium of Kinshasa who has done much research on the life and work of Adelmann, sums up three characteristics of his personality: "Adelmann was a cultivated man who had assimilated

---

[11] See Berengar, *Rescriptum contra Lanfrannum*, ed. R. B. C. Huygens, CCCM 84 (Turnhout: Brepols, 1988).

[12] On the letter to Hermann, see Hampe, "Reise nach England," 373–87.

[13] Clerval and Balau believed that they recognized Adelmann's style in a letter from Theoduinus of Liège to Henry I of France, but that letter dates from around 1051, when Adelmann had long since moved away from Liège (see Silvestre, "Notice sur Adelman de Liège," 862).

[14] Neither the *Stadtarchiv Speyer* nor the *Bistumsarchiv Speyer* nor the archive of the diocese of Brescia contains records on him.

[15] See Silvestre, "Notice sur Adelman de Liège," 863–4, based on the testimony of Bonizo, bishop of Sutri († ca. 1090), in his *Liber ad amicum*, mentioned in *Libelli de lite imperatorum et pontificum saeculis XI et XII conscripti*, ed. Ernst Dümmler et al., Monumenta Germaniae Historica, Libelli de lite 1 (Hanover: Hahnsche Buchhandlung, 1891), 593.

[16] Antoine Rivet de la Grange, *Histoire littéraire de la France*, vol. 7 (Paris: Firmin Didot/Treuttel et Wurtz, 1746), 546.

nearly all the knowledge a scholar could acquire at that time and in his situation. He had a gentle character and a heartfelt capacity for friendship. He was conservative in all domains. He cannot be considered a fanatical or primitive thinker. As is common in very good people, he was bold in the active life and humble in the intellectual. In short: he was an honest and good man, very knowledgeable, but not endowed with superior intelligence, nor with exceptional imagination."[17]

---

[17] Silvestre, "Notice sur Adelman de Liège," 864.

Introduction to the Texts

Letter from Adelmann to Berengar

Adelmann's letter to Berengar has been preserved in five manuscripts, two of which contain the complete text. Detailed descriptions of these five manuscripts can be found in R. B. C. Huygens's critical edition, which is reprinted, without change, in this volume.[1] The *editio princeps* of an abridged version seems to have been published by John Costerius (1515–1559), a regular canon of Saint Augustine. That edition is dated 1551. A second edition of the same abridgment was printed ten years later at the presses of John Vlimmerius († 1597). The first edition of the entire letter did not appear until 1770, when Conrad Arnold Schmidt rediscovered the complete text in a manuscript at the *Herzog-August-Bibliothek* at Wolfenbüttel.[2]

This affable missive can best be described as a short Eucharistic tract (*opusculum*) that agrees with Pascasius Radbertus's "realistic" interpretation concerning the sacraments of the Body and Blood of the Lord. The work was only moderately successful in its own time, but would be rediscovered during the Reformation. It remained somewhat popular during the seventeenth and eighteenth centuries, but after that time it all but sank into oblivion. Adelmann's letter owes its popularity to the fact that it was found useful by Catholics engaged in a Eucharistic controversy with Protestants. In the *Histoire littéraire de la France* by Antoine Rivet de la Grange it is even called "one of the nicest pieces of literature, in all aspects, from that time."[3]

Adelmann had previously reacted to Berengar's views in a letter, now no longer extant, to Paulinus, the *primicerius* of Metz. He had requested that Paulinus inquire into the exact nature of Berengar's views. It is probable, however, that Adelmann

---

[1] See Adelmann, "La lettre d'Adelman de Liège à Bérenger de Tours," in *Serta mediaevalia: Textus varii saeculorum X–XIII in unum collecti*, CCCM 171, ed. R. B. C. Huygens (Turnhout: Brepols, 2000), 166–201; also see R. B. C. Huygens, "Textes latins du XIe au XIIIe siècle," *Studi medievali. Serie terza* 8 (1967): 459–93.
[2] MS. Wolfenbüttel, *Herzog-August-Bibliothek*, 18.4. Aug. fol., fols. 116r–124v.
[3] Antoine Rivet de la Grange, *Histoire littéraire de la France*, vol. 7 (Paris: Firmin Didot/Treuttel et Wurtz, 1746), 547. On the use of Berengar and Adelmann in polemics against Protestantism, see Pontianus Polman, *L'élément historique dans la controverse religieuse au XVIe siècle* (Gembloux: Duculot, 1932).

received no answer from either Paulinus or Berengar. We know that Paulinus did correspond with Berengar, so it is unclear why Adelmann was not sent a reply.[4] In any case, his first letter is lost. We only have the two versions of his second letter to Berengar: the short and the long versions. We will discuss the longer version here.

The two manuscripts containing the entire text of the letter present us with a problem. In a postscript, we are told that Adelmann sent two letters to Berengar, the second being slightly longer than the first.[5] The story of the first letter is this: a certain brother G. (no more detailed identity is given) visited Adelmann. Adelmann gave him a letter to deliver to Berengar. However, G. was in such a hurry that Adelmann could not complete his important exposé on the tripartite Body of Christ. Apparently, Berengar did not answer this first letter, and therefore Adelmann decided to try again, with a longer letter. Research has shown that the longer version of the text preserved in the manuscripts is the same as that of the second, more complete letter. However, there is no basis for assuming that the shorter version of the text is the first letter.[6] Rather, it appears to be a later abridgment. Probably, then, both the short and the long text are both derived from the same, second letter. It is provisionally dated 1050–1051.[7]

The letter is structured chiastically[8]:

- personal greeting with a reminder and motivation;
- warning;
- the Body of Christ:

---

[4] See Jean de Montclos, *Lanfranc et Bérenger. La controverse eucharistique de XIe siècle*, Spicilegium sacrum Lovaniense. Études et documents 37 (Louvain: Peeters, 1971), esp. 12, 98–9, 127–8, and on the correspondence between Paulinus and Berengar: "Beringerius in purgatoria epistula contra Almannum," in *Thesaurus novus anecdotorum*, ed. Edmond Martène and Ursin Durand (Paris: F. Delaulne, H. Foucault, M. Clouzier, J.-G. Nyon, S. Ganeau, and N. Gosselin, 1717), vol. 4, col. 196.

[5] See "Letter from Adelmann to Berengar," p. 84 in this volume: "Epistolam eandem, sed paulo largiorem, ecce iam secundo tibi mitto, quoniam properante legato priore ropositam questionem de tripartita corporis Christi distinctione commode expedire copia non fuit. Credo etiam in manus tuas nondum illam pervenisse, nam si pervenisset nequaquam tam diu silentium tenuisses, maxime obsecratus a me per viscera misericordiae dei nostri, quod et nunc itero, ut quantotius rescriberes et evelleres ab animo meo scrupulum diu anxie que insidentem."

[6] Arguments for this can be found in "La lettre d'Adelman de Liège à Bérenger de Tours," ed. Huygens (see note 1 above), 169–75.

[7] See Jacob Van Sluis, "Adelman van Luik: De eerste opponent van Berengarius van Tours," *Nederlands theologisch tijdschrift* 47 (1993): 89–106, esp. 93. Montclos dates the letter to late 1052, but Van Sluis corrects this.

[8] See Van Sluis, "Adelman van Luik," 95.

1) in heaven;
2) in the Eucharist;
3) in the earthly Church;
- warning;
- personal greeting and blessing.

Adelmann begins his letter quite affably. He tries to ingratiate himself with Berengar by reminiscing about the time that they shared as students at Chartres and by calling Berengar his foster brother (*collectaneum*). Then Adelmann aims at a nerve by reminding him of the method that their teacher Fulbert ("our honourable Socrates") tried to instill in them: Fulbert encouraged his students to tread the royal path and follow diligently in the footsteps of the Church Fathers, to avoid getting mired in byways full of snares and obstacles. Adelmann is concerned about rumors that have reached him about his old schoolmate, who is said to have strayed from the righteous path concerning the Church's teachings on the Eucharist. Adelmann deliberately avoids the word "heresy." Adelmann then begs Berengar to keep the peace within the Christian community.

Adelmann's treatment of the sacraments of the Body and Blood of Christ (later called the Eucharist) is based on a tripartite distinction of the Body of Christ (*distinctio tripartita corporis Christi*). According to this distinction, the Body of Christ can manifest itself in three ways: as the historical body (the body that was born of the virgin Mary, that suffered, died, and was buried, and rose up to heaven); as the body of the Lord which is present during the sacrifice of the Mass; and finally as the body of Christ understood as the Church community. These three forms are distinct, but not separate. In the body that is the Eucharist, both of the other meanings are present as well: the Eucharist as a commemorative meal reminds us of the historical body of Christ, and as a communal meal, it anticipates the total Church, in which the faithful are united with their Lord. For Adelmann, the unity of the three manifestations of the *corpus Christi* is paramount.[9]

The discussion of the three manifestations of the Body of Christ begins with the refutation of a criticism. Considering the historical Body of Christ, Adelmann rejects the assumption that a priest could have the divine power to change bread and wine into the Body and Blood of Christ, just as the historical Christ changed water into wine at Canaan. Adelmann affirms that this metamorphosis takes place during the Eucharist, but it is not the priest who performs the miracle. In the administration of the sacrament, Christ Himself is at work.[10] Thus, one can only oppose what

---

[9] See ibid., 94.
[10] See ibid., 96.

would later be called the real presence if one does not believe in Christ or in the truth of His words. The universal meaning and truth of His words can hardly be doubted.[11] In the event, this problem has little to do directly with the controversy with Berengar.

In the discussion of the second manifestation, it again becomes clear that Adelmann has not yet read anything fundamental by Berengar. The discussion here certainly pertains to the controversy, but it cannot be said to constitute a direct response to Berengar's views: Adelmann analyzes the act of believing but hardly proves the real presence. In the extensive section on Christ's Body in the Eucharist, Adelmann must explain why the faithful cannot see that the bread and wine change into the Body and Blood. Not surprisingly, he turns to Holy Scripture: Paul himself states that the faithful depend on belief and not on perception (2 Cor. 5:7). Paul's definition of faith is the certainty about things one hopes for and the proof of things one cannot see (Hebr. 11:1). Adelmann places faith above sensory perception. Moreover, *ratio* does not have the capacity to comprehend the deepest mysteries of faith. The opposition between the visible and the invisible in the mysteries of faith cannot be understood by reason but can be taken only on trust.[12]

The third manifestation of Christ's Body, the Church, presents Adelmann with a paradox: how can the Body of Christ, which is in heaven, exist here on earth as something temporal (namely, bread) and even be susceptible to all kinds of corruption (including digestion by human stomachs)? If Christ only has one Body, how can bits and pieces of Him be present on different altars? Adelmann asserts that the fragmentation and the corruption within the Church as the Body of Christ are only temporary and that this does not contradict His glorified Body's presence in heaven.[13] In present-day terminology we would call this the problem of the mystical Body of Christ.

To counter Berengar's use of dialectics, Adelmann employs a different, and, according to him, more theological hermeneutic in order to penetrate the mysteries of faith. Adelmann distinguishes three mental functions. The first are the merely sensory functions (*sensus corporis*) such as hearing and seeing, which differ from both the sensory-spiritual functions (*sensus cum intellectu*), which include reading and writing, and from the purely spiritual function, which understands the *ratio* of numbers, the proportions of sounds, and all incorporeal concepts. Besides these sensory and spiritual functions, there is divine grace, which allows us to perceive God in an unmediated manner. This function is God's gift: faith (*fides*).

---

[11] See Josef Geiselman, *Die Eucharistielehre der Vorscholastik*, Forschungen zur christlichen Literatur- und Dogmengeschichte 15 (Paderborn: Schöningh, 1926), 304.
[12] See Van Sluis, "Adelman van Luik," 96–7.
[13] See ibid., 97–8.

The first two natural functions are incapable of comprehending the essence of the sacraments. This essence escapes both sensory and sensory-spiritual perception, so that it cannot be observed empirically. Only faith can regard both the internal and the supernatural. Adelmann cites baptism as an example: during a baptism the natural senses perceive only water, while faith realizes the true meaning of this sacramental event. The Eucharist is the same: only part of what happens during the sacrifice of Mass can be the object of natural perception. If there were a perceptible change in the species of bread and wine, the Eucharist would revert to a matter of natural perception, bypassing faith altogether. The sacrament does not show externally what is going on beneath the surface.[14]

The influence of Fulbert is apparent in Adelmann's letter and his emphasis on the importance of faith. Just like his teacher, Adelmann is convinced that the mysteries of faith cannot be completely comprehended by reason, because they transcend each of the human faculties. Only faith has total access to the revelation and to the integral understanding of the dogmas. Reason is only a function complementary to the senses, since it orders sensory data. Adelmann is not shy about admitting that he distrusts any and all judgements based on sensory perception and human experience. Faith is the only possible preparation for theological speculation, and the fundamentals of faith are best provided by Scripture and by the Church Fathers.[15] If Scripture tells us that Christ offers bread and wine as his Body and Blood, a true believer can hardly deny this.

With his far-reaching identification of the historical and the sacramental Body of Christ, Adelmann in fact goes beyond Fulbert, approaching the intuitions of Pascasius Radbertus. Fulbert was somewhat reserved about total identity.[16] To Adelmann, what would later be called the real presence is essential: for the sacrament to be effective, Christ's substantial presence in the sacrament must be beyond a doubt. The identification also solves another difficult question that was to persist long afterwards (among others, with Alger of Liège), namely, the question of the unworthy administrator (or receiver) of the sacrament of the Body and Blood of Christ. In order to answer this question, Adelmann resorts to the Augustinian distinction between the effectiveness and the validity of the sacrament. Adelmann is clear on this point: the state of grace that the administrator enjoys has no influence on the validity of the sacrament, since it is Christ who actually administers the sacrament through the mouth and hands of the priest. The priest cannot influence the truth of the sacrament.

---

[14] See Geiselman, *Die Eucharistielehre*, 303–04.
[15] See Ovidio Capitani, "Studi per Berengario di Tours," *Bullettino dell'Istituto storico Italiano per il medio evo e Archivo Muratoriano* 69 (1957): 67–173, esp. 104–05.
[16] See ibid., 105. Also see Fulbert's letter to Einhard in PL 141:192–6, and Geiselman, *Die Eucharistielehre*, 286–9.

Letter from Berengar to Adelmann

The surviving parts of Berengar's answer to Adelmann's letter were first published by Martène and Durand in their *Thesaurus novus anecdotorum*.[17] A critical edition did not appear until Montclos's *Lanfranc et Bérenger*; this is the edition that we reprint in this volume.[18] Both Martène/Durand and Montclos used a manuscript that once belonged to the Benedictine abbey Saints-Pierre-et-Exupère at Gembloux (Belgium) and is now kept in Brussels at the *Koninklijke Bibliotheek van België* (MS. 5576–604, fols. 161v–163r).[19] Berengar's answer to Adelmann's *opusculum* was apparently significantly less popular than Adelmann's *opusculum* itself, which was preserved in multiple manuscripts.

Berengar's epistle contains some mockery. After reading Adelmann's letter, he says, he felt as though "a ridiculous mouse was born" (*nascitur ridiculus mus*)—a quotation from Horace's *Ars poetica*.[20] The text also contains a mocking play on Adelmann's name: *Aulus mannus*, that is, Aulus the pony.[21] Berengar was known for his inflammatory personality, and his character plays an important part in the tone of this letter.

Berengar completely disagrees with Adelmann. This is quite apparent even from the mutilated version of the letter that remains. The letter is the only source we have on Berengar's views predating the Roman council of 1059 which condemned him. Berengar feels misunderstood and immediately states that he has no quarrel with the

---

[17] See "Beringerius in purgatoria epistula contra Almannum," in *Thesaurus novus anecdotorum*, ed. Edmond Martène and Ursin Durand (Paris: F. Delaulne, H. Foucault, M. Clouzier, J.-G. Nyon, S. Ganeau, and N. Gosselin, 1717), vol. 4, 109–14.

[18] See de Montclos, *Lanfranc et Bérenger* (cited in note 4 above), 531–9. For a review of this edition, see Hubert Silvestre, "Notes sur l'édition de l'épître de Bérenger de Tours à Adelman de Liège," *Recherches de théologie ancienne et médiévale* 49 (1972): 127–30.

[19] See Joseph Van den Gheyn, *Catalogue des manuscrits de la Bibliothèque royale de Belgique*, vol. 1 (Brussels: Henri Lamertin, 1901), no. 364.

[20] Strictly speaking, this text appears at the end of the *Rhythmus alphabeticus* (p. 108 below). However, in one of the two manuscripts of the *Rhythmus*—namely, MS. Brussels, *Koninklijke Bibliotheek van België*, 5576–604—the scribe does not appear to have recognised the *Rhythmus* as a work distinct from Berengar's letter to Adelmann. The frontispiece to this volume (p. vi) illustrates how the end of the letter and the beginning of the *Rhythmus* run together. At the end of the *Rhythmus* (!), the same manuscript reads, "Finit Beringerius contra Adelmannum" (p. 108 below). For the quotation from Horace, see Quinti Horati Flacci *Opera*, ed. David Roy Shackleton Bailey, Bibliotheca Scriptorum Graecorum et Romanorum Teubneriana (Stuttgart: Teubner, 1985), 316. The original quotation is, *nascetur ridiculus mus*. Context: do not begin with a grand opening like, "I shall sing of Priam," for what manner of grand things are there? The mountains will labor and a ridiculous mouse shall be born.

[21] "*Rhythmus alphabeticus*," p. 108 below.

doctrine according to which, through consecration, the bread and wine on the altar become the Body and Blood of Christ. Yet there are two important points where he deviates from Adelmann's position: the first is that Berengar claims that the transformation is perceived only by faith and the intellect; the second is that the transformation only affects the *res sacramenti* and not the *sacramentum*. The bread and wine on the altar of the Lord are changed into the Body and Blood of the Lord not *sensualiter* (by the senses) but *intellectualiter* (by the intellect), not by *absumptio* ("absumption," taking away) but by *assumptio* (assumption).[22]

At the heart of Berengar's reasoning is his use of the authority of Augustine. Knowing that the proper use of authorities is paramount for Adelmann, he quite accurately quotes six definitions of sacrament from the works of Augustine:[23]

1) *sacramentum, id est sacrum signum*, taken literally from *De civitate Dei* 10.5;[24]
2) *sacramentum est invisibilis gratiae visibilis forma*, based on *Epistola 105* 3.2;[25]
3) *sacramentum est divinae rei invisibilis signaculum visibile*, based on *De catechizandis rudibus* 26.50;[26]
4) *sacramentum est divini misterii signaculum*, based on *Sermo 351* (*De pœnitentia*);[27]
5) *non sunt aliud quaeque sacramenta corporalia nisi quaedam quasi verba visibilia, sacrosancta quidem, sed tamen mutabilia et temporalia*, from *Contra Faustum* 19.16;[28]
6) *sacrificia visibilia signa sunt invisibilium, sicut verba sonantia signa sunt rerum*, based on *De civitate Dei* 10.19.[29]

To clarify what a *signum* is, Berengar adds another Augustinian definition from *De doctrina christiana* 2.1.1: *Signum est res, praeter speciem quam ingerit sensibus, ex se faciens aliud aliquid in cogitationem venire*—"for a sign is a thing which of itself

---

[22] See Capitani, "Studi per Berengario di Tours," 110–11.
[23] For a short discussion of these quotations, see Geiselmann, *Die Eucharistielehre*, 294–5.
[24] Aurelius Augustinus, *De civitate Dei (libri I–X)*, ed. Bernardus Dombart and Alphonsus Kalb, CCSL 47 (Turnhout: Brepols, 1955), 277[15–16].
[25] Aurelius Augustinus, *Epistulae 31–123*, ed. Alois Goldbacher, CSEL 34.1 (Vienna: Tempsky, 1898), 604.
[26] Augustine, *Œuvres de Saint Augustin*, vol. 11: *Le magistère chrétien*, ed. Gustave Combès and Albert Farges, Bibliothèque augustinienne 11 (Paris: Desclée de Brouwer, 1949), 136.
[27] This sermon is spurious; see Pierre-Patrick Verbraken, *Études critiques sur les sermons authentiques de saint Augustin*, Instrumenta patristica 12 (Steenbrugge: in Abbatia S. Petri, 1976), esp. 147.
[28] Augustine, *De utilitate credendi, De duabus animabus, Contra Fortunatum, Contra Adimantum, Contra epistulam fundamenti, Contra Faustum*, ed. Iosephus Zycha, Corpus scriptorum ecclesiasticorum latinorum 25 (Vienna: Österreichische Akademie der Wissenschaften, 1891), 513[8–9].
[29] Augustine, *De civitate Dei (libri I–X)*, 293[4–5].

makes some other thing come to mind, besides the impression that it presents to the senses."[30] Berengar explains: *Non ait: In manum, in os, in dentem, in ventrem, sed: in cogitationem*—"he does not say, 'to the hands,' 'to the mouth,' 'to teeth,' 'to the belly,' but 'to the mind.'" These definitions are Berengar's pertinent contribution to sacramental theology. Up to that time, the definition by Isidore of Seville had been the most popular, but thanks to Berengar the Augustinian definition resurfaced. Many theologians had previously quoted Augustine's definitions, but had distorted their meaning to make them fit Isidore's.

As we have seen, Adelmann's letter revolved around the threefold character of the Body of Christ. Berengar does not respond to this premise, at least in the part of his answer that we still have. Likewise, he does not go into the question of unworthy administrators or receivers. Is it only these sections that have been lost from his original letter? We might presume that this is so; however, in much of the letter Berengar does not appear to be answering Adelmann's *opusculum* directly but rather to be formulating his own views. Unlike Adelmann, Berengar uses very compact language. The master from Tours does not focus on the three manifestations of Christ's Body, but on the distinction between *sacramentum* and *res sacramenti*, that is, the visible sign over against the invisible signified. The *sacramentum* is the visible sign (bread and wine) signifying the invisible *res sacramentum* (the Body and Blood of Christ).[31] Berengar deftly adds that he has borrowed this distinction from Augustine: a sacrament is a holy sign, and a sign is something that signifies something else. This reference delivers a riposte to Adelmann's accusation that he does not respect or use the authorities.

In the first part of the letter, Berengar does respond directly to two other reproaches from Adelmann. He claims that Adelmann has misunderstood him on two points. The first concerns the real presence of Christ in the Eucharist. Berengar maintains that Christ's historical Body is a reality (and not a seeming body) and that the bread and wine on the altar do indeed become the Body and Blood of Christ through consecration, though only for faith and intellect. Calling upon Augustine and Ambrose for evidence, the master from Tours secondly demonstrates that Christ presents himself on the altar only spiritually (*spiritualiter*) to the inner man. The signs of bread and wine are consumed bodily, but what they signify can be consumed spiritually only.[32]

---

[30] Translation: Augustine, *De doctrina Christiana*, trans. R. P. H. Green, Oxford Early Christian Texts (Oxford: Oxford University Press, 1995), 58.

[31] See Nicholas M. Häring, "Berengar's Definitions of *Sacramentum* and their Influence on Mediaeval Sacramentology," *Mediaeval Studies* 10 (1948): 109–46, and Damien Van den Eynde, *Les définitions des sacrements pendant la première période de la théologie scolastique (1050–1240)* (Rome: Antonianum; Louvain: Nauwelaerts, 1950), esp. 3–16.

[32] See Van Sluis, "Adelman van Luik," 99–100.

The third and final misunderstanding that Berengar must defuse is Adelmann's accusation that he interprets the Body and Blood as mere *figurae* (figures) and *similitudines* (semblances). This is why he introduces the distinction between *sacramentum* and *res sacramenti*: the *sacramenta* can indeed be interpreted as being figures or semblances, but not the *res sacramentorum*. Adelmann does not make this distinction and, to Berengar, this shows that he does not realize that it is by definition impossible for Christ's Body and Blood to be signs of Christ Himself. Not his Body and Blood, only the bread and wine can be signs, semblances, or substitutes. Not to realize this is evidence of the greatest folly.

He concludes with his central thesis: "My view, or rather that of the Scriptures, is this: the bread and the wine on the table of the Lord do not change visibly to the senses but intellectually, not by taking away (*per absumptionem*) but by assuming (*per assumptionem*). They do not change into a piece of meat (which contradicts Scripture) but completely into the Body and Blood of Christ (in accordance with Scripture)." A *res* can change through "absumption" or through "assumption." In the first case the transformation is total since one substance turns into another: the bread changes into meat. In the second case, the change is less radical: the substance of the bread is not destroyed but upgraded. The bread is elevated to a higher worth. In the *Rescriptum contra Lanfrannum*, Berengar describes this change as follows: "The bread that is consecrated on the altar has lost its imperfection and ineffectuality, but not its proper nature and with this nature as a basis and a foundation, its worth and effectiveness are enriched through God."[33] In the case of the Eucharist, the transformation can only be an assumption, since the bread and wine continue to look the same throughout. Opponents continue to speak of a substantial change, even though the external appearance remains the same. Berengar does believe change by absumption to be possible in other cases: for example, during the wedding at Canaan, where water became wine, or when Moses' staff turned into a snake.[34]

Letter from Adelmann to Hermann II of Cologne

The manuscript of the letter from Adelmann to Hermann II, archbishop of Cologne (1036–1052), is preserved at the British Library in London, where it bears the call number Add. 26788. It occupies fols. 91r–93r. The manuscript originated in the abbey of Deutz and dates back to the twelfth century. The first

---

[33] Beringerius Turonensis, *Rescriptum contra Lanfrannum*, ed. R. B. C. Huygens, CCCM 84 (Turnhout: Brepols, 1988), 84[1744–6].
[34] See Van Sluis, "Adelman van Luik," 101–02.

critical edition was prepared by Robert B. C. Huygens;[35] it is this edition that is reproduced in this volume. The content of the letter is of little interest theologically, but we include it to complete our edition of Adelmann's known works.

Rhythmus alphabeticus

As mentioned in Adelmann's biography, the first version of the song dates back to sometime between 1028 and 1033. The first version now resides at the *Kongelige Bibliotek* of Copenhagen, call number Gl. kgl. S. 1905, 4to, fols. 60v–61v. The volume of which it is a part also contains manuscripts of Boethius (*De consolatione*), Cicero (*De officiis*), Claudianus (*De raptu Proserpine*), a passion of Saint Agnes and of Saint Catherine, and some others. The manuscript was written at the end of the twelfth century or the beginning of the thirteenth. A fourteenth-century note on the manuscript says it belonged to the abbey of Affligem, the *novum monasterium* in Brabant.[36] This is the version that was published by Clerval, Havet, and MacKinney. In this volume, we have reprinted the edition by Havet.[37]

For a long time, however, only the second version of the poem was known. That version is preserved in a manuscript from the old monastery of Gembloux written at the end of the tenth or the beginning of the eleventh century. It was also the first edited version of the song. This version of the song is kept at the *Koninklijke Bibliotheek van België* in Brussels, MS. 5576–604. The verses Adelmann wrote are on fols. 163r and v, right after the fragment of Berengar's letter to Adelmann.[38] They have appeared in the editions of Mabillon, Martène and Durand, and Migne; in this volume, we have used Mabillon's text.[39]

---

[35] See "La lettre d'Adelman de Liège à Hermann II de Cologne," in *Serta mediaevalia. Textus varii saeculorum X–XIII in unum collecti*, ed. R. B. C. Huygens, CCCM 171 (Turnhout: Brepols, 2000), 202–08.

[36] For a description, see Ellen Jørgensen, *Catalogus codicum latinorum medii aevi Bibliothecae regiae Hafniensis* (Copenhagen: Gyldendals Forlag, 1926), pp. 334–5.

[37] See Jules Alexandre Clerval, *Les écoles de Chartres au moyen âge du Ve au XVIe siècle* (Paris: Picard, 1895; reprinted, Geneva: Slatkine, 1977), 59–61; Julien Havet, "Poème rythmique d'Adelman de Liège," *Notices et documents publiés par la Société de l'histoire de France à l'occasion du 50e anniversaire de sa foundation* (Paris: Renouard, 1884), 71–92; Loren C. MacKinney, *Bishop Fulbert and Education at the School of Chartres*, Texts and Studies in the History of Mediaeval Education 4 (Notre Dame, Ind.: Medieval Institute, 1957), 49–51. MacKinney made some corrections to Havet's critical edition.

[38] See Van den Gheyn, *Catalogue des manuscrits*, vol. 1 (cited in note 19 above), no. 364.

[39] For Mabillon's edition, see "Adelmanni scholastici Rythmi alphabetici de viris illustribus sui temopris," in *Vetera analecta sive collectio veterum aliquot operum et opusculorum omnis generis, carminum, epistolarum, diplomatum, epitaphiorum, etc.*, ed. Jean Mabillon, 2 vols. (Paris: Billaine, 1675–1676),

The two versions of the song are so dissimilar that their difference cannot be attributed to copying mistakes. We are clearly dealing with a case of editing by the author himself. The preamble to the Gembloux manuscript offers the key: Adelmann claims that he has rediscovered an old song, written by himself while he was still at Liège, and that he would like to send it to Berengar, but not without editing it first.[40] In the last verse of the Gembloux text, the edited version is situated in Speyer. Hence the following hypothesis: the song was first composed at Liège, while the revision occurred at Speyer.[41]

Unlike its documentary value, the literary value of the song is negligible. Adelmann mentions many biographical details about individuals from the first half of the eleventh century. Julien Havet has used this list to date the first version of the song, for in the Copenhagen version the author notes that all the people he mentions died within a period of five years. This note does not appear in the Brussels version; therefore, it must have been written after that five-year period ended. Fulbert died in 1028, so that the first version must have been completed sometime before 1033. The second, revised version is much more difficult to date. Havet conjectures it must have been composed sometime between 1040 and 1057.[42]

In both versions, the song pays homage to the twelve people whose passing Adelmann most regrets. First comes Fulbert, followed by seven of his students and finally four more inhabitants of Liège. The two versions have nine names in common. Three names from the first version do not occur in the second version and are replaced by three other names. Two of these replacements could, however, also have been caused by scribal error.[43]

The song is written in a rhythmic meter quite popular in the Middle Ages. Each verse counts fifteen syllables, divided over the two halves of the verse (eight and seven syllables). The seventh and the thirteenth syllable of each verse (that is, the next to last syllable of the first half of the verse and the second to last syllable of the second half of the verse) are accentuated. Otherwise, the accent usually falls on uneven syllables, but this is not obligatory. A hiatus is allowed, and very few vowels are elided (unless the final vowel of a word does not fit

---

1:420–5; new edition (more widely available) under the same title (Paris: Montalant, 1723), 382–3; reprint of this new edition (Farnborough, Hants.: Gregg Press, 1967). For the edition by Martène and Durand, see *Thesaurus novus anecdotorum*, ed. Edmond Martène and Ursin Durand (see note 17 above), vol. 4, 113–14. For Migne's reprint of Mabillon's edition, see PL 143:1295–8.

[40] See "Rhythmus alphabeticus," p. 104 below in this volume.
[41] See Havet, "Poème rythmique" (note 37 above), 77.
[42] See ibid., 77–8.
[43] See ibid., 78.

the vowel at the beginning of the next word). The manuscript from Copenhagen has three elisions: once an *e* before another *e* or *æ* and twice an *i* before another *i*. In the other manuscript there are three cases of an *e* left out and not a single *i*.[44]

The *Rhythmus* is divided into stanzas of three verses that rhyme with each other. Each of these tercets Adelmann calls a verse (*versus*). The stanzas form an alphabetical series. The first tercet starts with an A, the second with a B, and so forth, until the last, the twenty-third, which begins with a Z. The first tercet points out that the stanzas should actually be sung, and indeed the Copenhagen manuscript includes neumes. This is why we call it Adelmann's "song" and not his "poem." The song lacks all literary charm, and most of it is quite difficult to interpret. Several tercets that were badly constructed in the first version are revised in the second version.

Several commentators have argued that verse 18,3 includes an allusion to the simony of the bishop of Liège, Reginard, but there are two important counterarguments.[45] In the first place, there is no historical evidence that Reginard bought his bishopric; in the second place, it is highly unlikely that Adelmann would allude to simony committed by his own bishop, let alone while he was still living in Liège. Verse 18,3 can be very broadly interpreted, and there is no binding reason to view it as a reproach of Reginard.[46] It is true that Adelmann does not always tread carefully, as is apparent from his letter to archbishop Herman II of Cologne. Jules Alexandre Clerval has endeavored to bring some structure into Adelmann's list.[47]

---

[44] See ibid., 79.
[45] This older view can be found in Sylvain Balau, *Les sources de l'histoire de Liège au moyen âge. Étude critique* (Brussels: H. Lamertin, 1903), 161; Max Manitius, *Geschichte der lateinischen Literatur des Mittelalters*, 3 vols. (Munich: Beck, 1911–1931), 2:558 n. 3 and 2:561; and Wilhelm Wattenbach, *Deutschlands Geschichtsquellen im Mittelalter. Deutsche Kaiserzeit*, ed. Robert Holtzmann, 4 vols. (Berlin: Ebering, 1938–1943), 718 n. 246.
[46] See Hubert Silvestre, "Adelman," in *Biographie nationale publiée par l'Académie royale des sciences, des lettres et des beaux-arts de Belgique*, vol. 33: *Supplément* (Brussels: Bruylant, 1965), 1–8, at 2, and Hubert Silvestre, *Le "Chronicon Sancti Laurentii Leodiensis" dit de Rupert de Deutz*, Recueil de travaux d'histoire et de philologie, 3ᵉ série, 43 (Louvain: Publications universitaires, 1952), 228–31 and 264–5.
[47] See Clerval, *Les écoles de Chartres* (note 37 above), 58–93.

MS. Copenhagen, *Kongelige Bibliotek*, Gl. kgl. S. 1905, 4ᵗᵒ, fol. 60v. By kind permission of the Royal Library, Copenhagen.

MS. Copenhagen, *Kongelige Bibliotek*, Gl. kgl. S. 1905, 4to, fol. 61r. By kind permission of the Royal Library, Copenhagen.

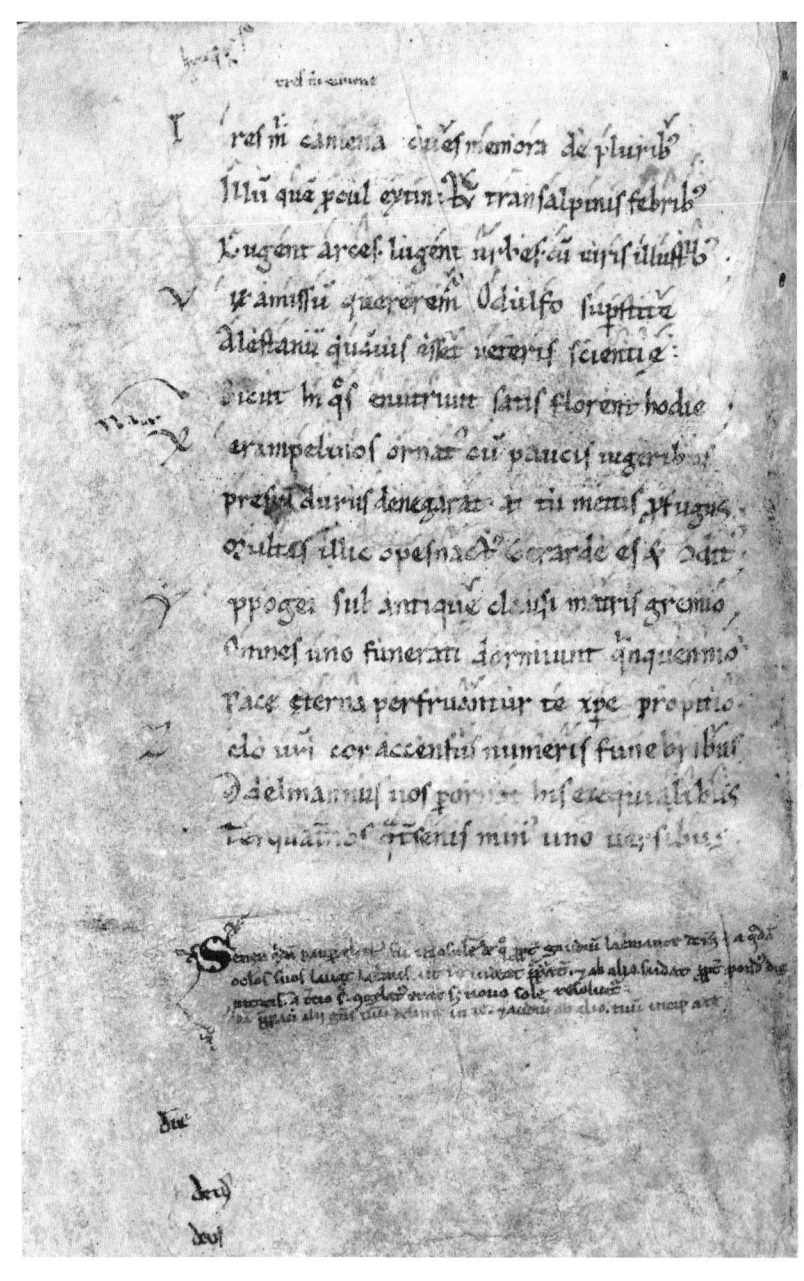

Introduction to the Texts 55

MS. Copenhagen, *Kongelige Bibliotek*, Gl. kgl. S. 1905, 4to, fol. 61v. By kind permission of the Royal Library, Copenhagen.

The Neumes of Adelmann's *Armonice facultatis* in the Copenhagen Manuscript
(by Pieter Mannaerts[48])

Adelmann's *Armonice facultatis*, an abecedary in rhythmic verse (*rhythmicos versiculos*), was copied into the Copenhagen manuscript in a version that contains both text and music. Even though the abbreviations occasionally seem to hinder a fluent reading of the neumes,[49] the page layout and ink quality suggest that both text and music were written at the same time, possibly even by the same scribe. The theoretical possibility exists that the music was added later to the original poem (and its original manuscript) and that both were then copied simultaneously into the Copenhagen manuscript. This is unlikely, however, as it would seem rather irrelevant to an author other than Adelmann to add music to a text as autobiographical as *Armonice facultatis*. It may thus be assumed that the poem was conceived as a musical whole from the outset.

In the following, the parameters that may contribute to a fuller understanding of *Armonice facultatis* as a musical composition will be briefly considered.

The Copenhagen manuscript shows neumes *in campo aperto*, that is, written in a space without ruled horizontal lines. More precisely, the neumes are adiastematic accent (or stroke) neumes, indicating both the melodic direction (ascending or descending intervals) and the number of tones. The neumes do not, however, indicate precise pitches. As a consequence, a full transcription is impossible without reliance on concordant diastematic sources. Unfortunately, such a source for *Armonice facultatis* is unknown to date.

Since no other musical sources are available, a closer look at the poetic genre could lead us further. In *Armonice facultatis*, the rhythmic poetry and its text-setting style (see below) suggest a composition that may be similar to hymns and sequences, two types of medieval rhythmic poetry that were commonly set to music.

The sequence-type of composition can be excluded from consideration. Although the arrangement of the text lines in groups of 8 + 7 syllables is rather common in sequence texts, *Armonice facultatis* does not correspond to the basic sequence structure, which consists of paired versicles set to an identical melody, mostly preceded and followed by a single versicle ("a-bb-cc-*etc.*-z"). The exceptions to this general rule are either notably shorter and of an earlier date than Adelmann's composition, or of Italian origin.[50]

---

[48] Pieter Mannaerts is postdoctoral research fellow at the *Katholieke Universiteit Leuven*. He wishes to thank Susan Boynton, Ike de Loos, Barbara Haggh-Huglo, and Nils Holger Petersen for their helpful comments on earlier drafts of this text.
[49] For example, at *verborum* in the E-stanza.
[50] See David Hiley, *Western Plainchant: A Handbook* (Oxford: Clarendon Press, 1991), 172–95.

The hymn repertory, on the other hand, is a relatively small one. In view of the strophic form and metrical regularity of hymns, it is almost self-evident that contrafacting eventually became a common practice in the genre.[51] In spite of these features, however, several elements complicate the retrieval of a melody matching the text in the case of Adelmann's composition. Although it is not impossible that a cleric such as Adelmann would take a liturgical melody as a model to set a newly written, non-liturgical text to music, it would be rather exceptional to find a contrafact in a poem as original and autobiographical as *Armonice facultatis*. Furthermore, contrafacting was very common from the thirteenth century on, but this was not yet the case at the time of Adelmann's composition. By virtue of its content, Adelmann's abecedary is a non-liturgical work. Consequently, it comes as no surprise that a brief comparison to melodies in both the *Liber hymnarius*[52] and Stäblein's *Hymnen*[53] yielded no matches. Finally, there is the problem of the accessibility of the sources: only a relatively small number of them—both those containing the internationally disseminated part of the hymn repertory and those containing the local sources—have been published. To date, no research has been conducted on the hymn repertoire of the Liégeois area.

Nevertheless, the absence of the actual melody does not imply that the musical identity of *Armonice facultatis* remains a closed book altogether. The neumes give valuable indications of the importance of the source, of the relation of text and music, and of the manuscript's area of origin and its content.

As a rule, only the first strophe of a hymn is notated, since it is a strophic composition and normally has the same melody for each stanza. Only a few exceptions are known in which entire hymn texts have musical notation.[54] Adelmann's hymn in the Copenhagen manuscript seems to be one of them, as it has neumatic notation throughout its 23 stanzas. Consequently, the manuscript may be considered a remarkable musical source from a palaeographic point of view.

Armonice facultatis displays typical hymn characteristics such as strophic form and metrical regularity. Its text setting is mainly in syllabic and neumatic style.[55] Three

---

[51] See ibid., 140–8.
[52] See *Liber hymnarius cum invitatoriis & aliquibus responsoriis*, Antiphonale Romanum secundum liturgiam horarum, tomus alter (Solesmes: Abbaye Saint-Pierre de Solesmes, 1983).
[53] See Bruno Stäblein, *Hymnen*, 1: *Die mittelalterlichen Hymnenmelodien des Abendlandes*, Monumenta monodica medii aevi 1, 2nd ed. (Kassel: Bärenreiter, 1995).
[54] Susan Boynton, "Hymn, II: Monophonic Latin," in *The New Grove Dictionary of Music and Musicians*, ed. Stanley Sadie and John Tyrell, 2nd ed. (London: Macmillan, 2001), 12:19–23, cites as examples I-Rvat S Pietro B 79, I-FRa A 209 (Farfa, 11th century), and E-H 1 (southern France, 11th century).
[55] The term "neumatic" in the context of style means "containing two to four notes per syllable," as opposed to "syllabic" (one note per syllable) and "melismatic" (many notes per syllable) styles.

of the verse halves (1a, 1b, 2a) have a *pes* on the final syllable. The end of the second verse has a small cadence of 4 + 2 + 3 notes to its last three syllables, in most cases written as *pes subbipunctis—clivis— climacus*. As is often the case in hymn melodies, the multiple note groups do not coincide with the text accents. Variation and repetition of short segments within one line of melody or between different lines are common features of many hymns. Accordingly, a melodic similarity of verse halves 1a and 2a is suggested by the neumes of *Armonice facultatis*.

The study of the neumatic type usually provides relatively strong indications as to the provenance of musical sources. A closer investigation of the type used in *Armonice facultatis* may shed a new light on Havet's assertion that Adelmann's poem was composed in Liège rather than Speyer.[56]

Western neumatic notations are generally classified into a number of groups of more or less uniform and consistent types of notation. These types, such as "German," "French," "Aquitanian," "Lorraine," etc., are used over a relatively large geographic area. Solange Corbin introduced the concept of "contact neumes,"[57] to refer to those neumatic notations that use elements from two or more of the groups mentioned.

The neumes in Adelmann's *Armonice facultatis* can be classified as a contact form of German and French neumes. Ike de Loos has termed these contact neumes "Low Countries notation."[58] Generally, these contact neumes take elements from German and French notations, as follows:[59]

- The *clivis* has a round form (as in German neumes);
- the *pes* has an angular form (as in French notation);
- the *climacus* angle ranges from rather wide (German) to rather narrow (French);
- on average, the axis of notation is rather narrow (French);

---

[56] See Havet, "Poème rythmique" (note 37 above), 74–5.
[57] See Solange Corbin, *Die Neumen*, Palaeographie der Musik I, 3 (Cologne: Arno Volk, 1977).
[58] Josine Francisca Helena [Ike] de Loos, *Duitse en Nederlandse muzieknotaties in de 11de en 12de eeuw* (diss. University of Utrecht, 1996), esp. 72–92.
[59] It may be useful to elucidate some neumatic nomenclature here. *Virga*, *punctum*, *tractulus*, *gravis*, and *uncinus* are signs used to indicate a single tone. A *pes* is a neume of two ascending tones; *clivis* is its descending counterpart. A *torculus* is a three-tone neume, consisting of a downward movement, followed by an upward one; *porrectus* is its inversion. *Climacus* is a succession of at least three descending notes; *scandicus* is its ascending version. *Pes subbipunctis* is a *pes* followed by two descending notes. *Oriscus* and *quilisma* are single-tone neumes with a debated rhythmic, melodic, or vocal significance; *pressus* is a particular form of neume involving the *oriscus* sign. *Strophici* are signs for repeated notes. "Liquescence" is the modification of form for the sake of pronunciaton. Significative letters and *episemata* are additional signs that modify the rhythmic, melodic, or vocal significance of the neumes to which they apply. See Hiley, *Western Plainchant*, 340–401; Corbin, *Die Neumen*, 1–11; Eugène Cardine, *Sémiologie grégorienne*, Études grégoriennes 11 (Solesmes: Abbeye de Solesmes, 1970).

- the *torculus* is used very sparingly, and its first element is round (German);
- single-tone neumes have several different forms: *virga* and *punctum* predominate (German and French);
- in contrast to *torculus* and *pes*, the *pes subbipunctis* has both angular (French) and round forms (German).

A full assessment of the notation of the melody of a single hymn is not an obvious task. Since the same melody is used for each stanza, it uses only a limited number of neume forms. Although the number of variants in the notation is considerable, yielding a few instances of *tractulus* ("*scientie*" in the E-stanza), *gravis* ("*am*nes" in the G-stanza), and liquescent neumes, which are not found in the first stanza, the neumatic picture still remains incomplete. More specifically, there are no instances of *scandicus*, *oriscus*, *pressus*, *strophici*, or *quilisma*. Neither do significative letters or *episemata* occur.

The neumes show similarities to two of the sub-groups defined by de Loos. They match most closely the neumes of de Loos's groups 1 and 3. The former covers notation forms from Liège and its surroundings, dated before 1100, showing a stronger French than German influence. The latter is found in manuscripts that originated after 1100 within the triangle Trier—Stavelot—Utrecht (including Liège), and displays more German characteristics, such as a more ample spacing of the neumes and a tendency to slope towards the right.

One more important element should be mentioned: *Armonice facultatis* often uses an *uncinus*-shaped neume to represent a single tone. It occurs both in its normal and in its enlarged form.[60] The *uncinus* is the distinguishing feature of a third notation group, the Lorraine neumes.

Since "at all periods, there was a close alliance between Lorraine and the area corresponding to modern Belgium, which borrowed its notation from Lorraine,"[61] the presence of an element of Lorraine notation cannot be called surprising, nor should it be interpreted as pointing to a different area of origin. On the contrary, several manuscripts in full Lorraine notation from the region have been preserved, notably the missals Brussels, *Koninklijke Bibliotheek van België*, II 3822, from the Liège

---

[60] Luigi Agustoni and Johannes Berchmans Göschl, *Einführung in die Interpretation des Gregorianischen Chorals*, I: *Grundlagen* (Regensburg: Bosse, 1987), 172, state that the diminished form is far more currently used than its enlarged counterpart, and that the *uncinus* is not normally repeated several times, certainly not in its enlarged form. It seems clear that the Copenhagen manuscript, in which the diminished form does not, and repetitions do frequently occur, makes atypical use of the *uncinus* neume.

[61] Solange Corbin, "Neumatic Notations," in *The New Grove Dictionary of Music and Musicians*, ed. Stanley Sadie (London: Macmillan, 1980), 13:137.

diocese,[62] and Brussels, *Koninklijke Bibliotheek van België*, 2031–2032, from the Stavelot-Malmédy region. The first manuscript, dating from ca. 1100, has Low Countries neumes in some places (fols. 11, 15, and 78), the second dates presumably from the eleventh century.[63]

Regarding the type of neumatic notation, it may be concluded that it attests to the origin from a region in which multiple palaeographic influences can be observed. This multitude of influences has so far not been demonstrated for Speyer and its surroundings; manuscripts from this area would probably use German neumes rather than Lorraine or French ones. Moreover, as Adelmann probably received his (musical) education in Liège, he would normally have made use of the predominant regional types of notation. The oldest sources containing the Low Countries' notation originated in Liège, the diocese which furthermore witnessed the introduction of Lorraine notation and the occurrence of both notation types in manuscripts, such as Brussels II 3822. If it is assumed that the Copenhagen manuscript was copied faithfully from its original, its notation, as a contact form of Low Countries and Lorraine neumes, can thus be considered to corroborate Havet's hypothesis that *Armonice facultatis* originated in the region around Liège.[64]

---

[62] The flyleaf carries the note: "Monasterium s. Huberti Andaginensis in diocesis Leodiensis."
[63] See Ike de Loos, "Chant behind the dikes," http://utopia.ision.nl/users/ikedl/chant.
[64] See note 56 above.

The Texts

Adelmanni de veritate corporis et sanguinis Domini in Eucharistia ad Berengarium epistola

Dilecto in Christo fratri conscolastico atque conlactaneo Berengario Adelmannus salutem in domino.

 Conlactaneum te meum vocavi propter dulcissimum illud contubernium, quod te cum adolescentulo, ipse ego maiusculus, in achademia Carnotensi sub nostro illo venerabili Socrate iocundissime duxi, cuius de convictu gloriari nobis dignius licet quam gloriabatur Plato, gratias agens naturae eo, quod in diebus Socratis sui hominem se et non pecudem peperisset. Nos enim sanctiorem vitam salubrioremque doctrinam catholici et christianissimi viri una experti sumus, et nunc eius apud deum precibus adiuvari sperare debemus: neque enim putandus est memoriam, in qua nos tanquam in sinu materno semper ferebat, amisisse, aut vero caritas Christi, qua sicut filios amplectebatur, in eo extincta est, sed absque dubio memor nostri et diligens plenius, quam cum in corpore mortis huius peregrinaretur, invitat ad se votis et tacitis precibus, obtestans per secreta illa et vespertina colloquia, quae nobis cum in hortulo iuxta capellam de civitate illa, quam deo volente senator nunc possidet, sepius habebat, et obsecrans per lacrimas, quas, interdum in medio sermone prorumpens, exundante sancti ardoris impetu emanabat, ut illuc omni studio properemus, viam regiam directim gradientes, sanctorum patrum vestigiis observantissime inherentes, ut nullum prorsus [in] diverticulum, nullam in novam et fallacem semitam desiliamus, ne forte in laqueos et scandala incidamus, quia, sicut ait psalmista, *iuxta iter scandalum posuerunt mihi*. Nam quod est iuxta iter, hoc est extra iter. De via autem quid dicit? *Pax multa diligentibus legem tuam, et non est illis scandalum*. Et quid est lex domini nisi via domini? Sicut in alio psalmo cantatur: *viam mandatorum tuorum cucurri, cum dilatasti cor meum*. Ergo in via pax, extra viam scandalum. Hoc scandalum incurrunt qui, per hereses et scismata deviantes, pacem catholicam impiis contentionibus rescindunt. Quos nihilominus in psalmo XIII° ita notatos advertimus: *contritio et infelicitas in viis eorum, et viam pacis non cognoverunt*. Ecce scandalum vel potius scandala, nempe contritio et infelicitas aeterna, quae occurrunt in semitis hereticorum viam pacis catholicae nosse recusantium. Avertat dominus a te, sancte frater, tales semitas et convertat pedes tuos in testimonia sua et mendaces ostendat qui famam tuam tam faeda labe maculare nituntur, spargentes usquequaque, ut non solum

Adelmann's Letter to Berengar,
on the Reality of the Body and Blood of the Lord in the Eucharist

Adelmann to his beloved brother in Christ, fellow teacher and foster brother Berengar: greetings in the Lord's name.

I have called you my foster brother because of that most pleasant friendship I so much enjoyed when you were yet young and I was your elder, at the academy of Chartres under our venerable Socrates,[1] in whose company we can take more pride than did Plato, when he thanked nature for making him a man, not a beast, in the days of his Socrates.[2] For we were exposed to the holy life and salubrious doctrine of a Catholic and Christian man, and now we must hope to be helped by his prayers before God. But we must not dream that the memory in which he always kept us as if at a mother's breast is lost, or suppose that the love of Christ, in which like sons he embraced us, is extinguished in him. Without a doubt, he remembers us still and loves us even more than when he was exiled here below in his mortal body, and with wishes and silent prayer he calls us to him, imploring us in the name of those secret evening conversations which he often had with us in the garden next to that chapel at Chartres which is now owned by the senator, through God's will. In tears, which he used to weep in the middle of a conversation and which he freely let flow in a fit of holy ardor, he begs us to hurry diligently there, to go directly by the king's road,[3] carefully following the footsteps of the holy Fathers, so that we do not lose our way or embark on a new and treacherous path, or stumble upon snares and traps.[4] As the psalmist says: *Beside my path they have set a trap.*[5] Beside the path, of course, is not on the path. But what does he say about the road? *There is great peace for those who follow your law, and there is no trap for them.*[6] And what is the law of the Lord other than the road of the Lord? As another psalm tells us: *I have followed the path of your commandments, and you have enlarged my mind.*[7] So there is peace on the road and a trap off the road. "They fall into this trap who deviate into heresy and schisms,"[8] and disrupt the Catholic peace[9] with godless contentions. We note the following about them in psalm 13: *Sadness and contrition cross their path, and they do not know the way of peace.*[10] You see, the trap or rather the traps, and certainly eternal sadness and penitence, occur on the byways of the heretics, who refuse to recognize the road of Catholic peace. May the Lord keep such byways from you, holy brother, and may He turn your footsteps toward his testament:[11] and may He expose as liars those who would befoul your good name with their false tongues, repeating everywhere, not just to the French, but also the Germans (among whom I have been away for some time) that you have abandoned the unity of our holy Mother Church and that you seem to differ from what the Catholic faith knows concerning the Body and the Blood of our Lord, which is offered daily upon the

Latinas, verum etiam Teutonicas aures, inter quos iam diu peregrinor, repleverint, quasi te ab unitate sanctae matris aecclesiae divulseris et de corpore ac sanguine domini, quod cottidie in universa terra super sanctum altare immolatur, aliter quam fides catholica teneat sentire videaris, hoc est, ut illorum de te dictis utar, non esse verum corpus Christi neque verum sanguinem, sed figuram quandam et similitudinem.

Haec ante hoc biennium cum audissem, fraternitatem tuam per epistolam convenire idque ex te ipso certius sciscitandum esse decrevi. Sciens porro familiarem tuum domnum Paulinum, Metensem primicerium, tibi propiorem mihique aliquanto viciniorem esse, ex mea petitione et sua pollicitatione delegavi sibi huius negotii executionem. At ille (non enim in hac re laudare eum possum, neglegens sive alterutrum sive utrumque nostrum, usque adhuc reliquit me suspensum. Sed divina gratia nos nunquam neglegens inopinato mihi optulit melius quam optabam. Optabam autem invenire hominem peregrinandi usu exercitatum, regionis et linguae Francorum non ignarum, et ecce stetit mihi e latere frater iste G., ex tuo nomine me salutans. Obstupui pre gaudio, et tamen non potui, fateor, tam repentino eventui fidem integram habere, quia frater idem nullum abs te signum litteratorium, uti mos est inter amicos tam longe remotos tamque diu non visos, afferebat, quod tamen ipsum multis de causis facile persuasibilibus excusabat. Sive ergo vere sive aliter hoc agebat, ego eum a domino preparatum mihi esse non diffidens, nolui diutius dissimulare quin ipse mente ac spiritu meo, presentibus litteris tanquam pennis induto, per tanta terrarum spacia transvolarem, obsecrans per misericordiam dei, per suavissimam memoriam Folperti, ut pacem catholicam diligas neque conturbes rem publicam christianae civitatis bene iam compositam a maioribus nostris, pro qua tot milia martyrum contra idolatriam et regnum diaboli fortiter certantes triumphaverunt, subindeque sancti doctores bella civilia ab hereticis commota salutaris eloquentiae fluminibus restinxerunt, itaque eam circumquaque munierunt, ut iam novus hostis nullus oboriri queat, qui, adversus eam aliquid nitens, non continuo mille iaculis desuper ruentibus obruatur. Ideo confusi sunt omnes et defecerunt. Ubi enim sunt Manichei? Ubi Arriani? Quonam tota illa factio perditissimorum civium evasit? Conputruit etiam memoria eorum. At vero Ambrosius, Augustinus, Hieronimus et alii plures bestiarum talium oppressores cum laudibus vivunt cottidieque splendidius efflorescunt.

Bonum est, frater, nobis parvulis sub istorum ducum titulis delitescere, quorum tam valida tamque probabilis est apud aecclesiasticas aures auctori-

holy altar throughout the world—which is (to use their words about you) that it is not the true Body of Christ, nor His true Blood, but a kind of form or likeness.

When I first heard this some two years ago, I decided to write a letter and approach you as a brother, in an attempt to obtain more dependable information from you yourself. Then, since I knew that your close friend, his lordship Paulinus, *primicerius* of Metz, lives close to you and is more or less a neighbor, I assigned to him, after asking him and obtaining his promise, the task of following the matter up. However, he (and I cannot praise him for his conduct[12]) has left me in suspense, neglecting either one of us or both of us. But the divine grace that never abandons us came to my aid unlooked for, more than I could have wished. I was hoping to find a man, a practiced traveler, who was well acquainted with the region and the language of the French, and suddenly at my side appeared Brother G., greeting me in your name. I stood transfixed with joy, but had some trouble accepting this sudden occurrence with complete faith, since this brother had brought no written token at all from you (as is customary among friends who are so far away from each other and have not seen each other for so long). For this he apologized, giving many and very convincing excuses. Either he was being honest in this or he was not, but I did not doubt he had been provided to me by the Lord.[13] I therefore did not wish to disguise any longer that I would fly myself in mind and spirit across so great an earthly space, wearing this letter like wings,[14] and begging you by the compassion of God and by the sweet memory of Fulbert to foster the Catholic peace,[15] and not disturb the affairs of the Christian state so well established by our forefathers.[16] So many thousands of martyrs triumphed on that state's behalf in the brave fight against idolatry and the reign of the devil. Soon after, our saintly wise men extinguished the civil wars instigated by the heretics with rivers of salvific eloquence, and they so fortified her on all sides that no new enemy[17] could present himself who would not, if he attempted anything against her, be forthwith buried under a deluge of objections. This is why they are all confounded and have given up.[18] Where now are the Manichaeans? Where are the Arians? Where has this whole movement of utterly lost people disappeared to? Even their memory has rotted away.[19] But Ambrose, Augustine, Jerome, and several others who subdued such animals live on with praise, and every day their splendor grows.

It is good, my brother, for us who are so small, to shelter behind the fame of those leaders, whose authority, overwhelming in the brilliance of its holy virtues and the

tas, sanctarum virtutum fulgore et caelestis sapientiae luce prepollens, ut extremae iam sit dementiae vel de ratione fidei vel de ordine recte vivendi eis in aliquo refragari. Quare? Nonne homines erant et falli ab aliis atque ipsi fallere alios poterant? Ita enim dicit Scriptura verax, quia *omnis homo mendax*. Unde ergo eo culminis pervenerunt, ut tam ratum habendum sit quicquid de divinis mysteriis senserunt memoriaeque mandaverunt? Nam et gentiles magni quidam et nobiles philosophi multa falsa, quae iure contempnimus, non solum de creatore deo, sed et de hoc mundo et de his quae in eo sunt sensisse inveniuntur. Quid enim absurdius affirmari potest quam caelum astraque omnia stare, terram vero rapida vertigine in medio circumferri, falli vero eos qui putent caelestia moveri, quemadmodum falluntur navigantes quibus turres atque arbores cum ipsis littoribus recedere videntur, solem preterea non calere, nivem nigram esse, audire quis ferat? Sunt apud illos plura aeque monstruosa, quae persequi longum est et nugatorium. De quibus doctor noster: *dicentes*, inquit, *se esse sapientes stulti facti sunt*.

Non hos elegit dominus qui, superbiae inflati spiritu, evanuerunt in cogitationibus suis. At nostri illi patres, humiles corde ac pauperes spiritu, pro quibus Salvator patrem glorificat hoc modo: *confiteor tibi, pater, domine caeli et terrae, quia abscondisti haec a sapientibus et prudentibus et revelasti ea parvulis*, ideo veraces sunt, quia participaverunt et coheserunt illi qui ait: *Ego sum via et veritas et vita*. A quo etiam intus didicerunt quod de sacramento hoc, quo de agimus, foris docuerunt. Audierunt enim eum de se ipso in evangelio ita predicantem: *Ego sum panis vivus qui de caelo descendi. Si quis manducaverit ex hoc pane, vivet in aeternum, et panis, quem ego dabo, caro mea est pro mundi vita*.

"Dabo," inquit, non ait "dedi." Quando ergo dare cepit? Quando pridie quam pateretur accepit panem et elevatis oculis in caelum gratias agens benedixit ac fregit et dedit discipulis suis, dicens: *accipite et comedite, hoc est corpus meum*. Similiter et calicem postquam cenavit, dicens: accipite et bibite ex eo omnes. Hic est calix sanguinis mei, qui pro vobis et pro multis effundetur in remissionem peccatorum. Quis hoc ita esse non credit, nisi qui aut Christo non credit aut ipsum hoc dixisse non credit? Sed de incredulis nihil ad nos. Dixisse autem hoc Christum testes non duo tantum aut tres, in quibus stat omne verbum, sed quatuor certissimi probatissimique existunt, duo scilicet ex circumcisione et duo ex preputio, ut uterque populus suis ac legitimis auctoritatibus sive ad salutem sive ad iudicium uteretur. Dixit utique,

light of its heavenly wisdom, is so potent and pleasing to ecclesiastical ears, that it would be extremely foolish to challenge them in any way either on the doctrines of faith or on the right way of life. Why? Were they not human, and could they not be deceived by others or themselves deceive? Scripture, which does not lie, says as much, *since all men are liars.*[20] Have they reached such a height that all they believed about divine mysteries and all that they passed on into tradition must be considered correct? For some of the great heathens and the noble philosophers are found to have believed many things that were wrong, and which we rightly condemn, not only about God, our creator, but also about the world and what is in it.[21] For what could be more absurd than to claim that the sky and all the stars are immobile, while the earth is spinning around by a rapid movement in its center?— and that they who think the sky is moving are deceived,[22] just as seafarers are deceived when they seem to see towers and trees receding with the coastline? Who could bring himself to agree that the sun is not hot, or "that snow is black"?[23] Among them, many such fallacies abide, and it would take too long and be a waste of time to list them all. Our teacher says this about them: *They claimed to be wise, but became foolish.*[24]

The Lord did not choose these[25] because, in a spirit of inflated superiority, they became futile in their thinking.[26] But those leaders of ours who were humble of heart and poor in spirit,[27] and for whom our Savior praised his Father thus: *I profess to you, Father, Lord of heaven and earth, that you have kept these things hidden from the wise and intelligent, and revealed them to the least of men,*[28] these Fathers tell the truth because they shared with and stayed with the one who says: *I am the way and the truth and the life.*[29] From this they learned inside what they taught outside of the sacrament under discussion here.[30] For they heard Him who proclaims of Himself in the Gospel: *I am the living bread who came down out of heaven. If anyone eats of this bread, he will live forever, and the bread that I shall give is my flesh, for the life of the world.*[31]

"I shall give," He says, and not "I have given." When, then, did He start giving? It was when, the day before the Passion, He took the bread and said thanks for it with his eyes turned toward heaven, broke the bread, and passed it to his disciples, saying: *Take this and eat it, this is my body.* Then, after eating, He did the same with the wine cup, saying: "Take this cup and drink from it, all of you. This is my blood, which will be poured out for you and for many for the remission of sins."[32] Who does not believe this, except someone who does not believe in Christ, or that He said these words? But unbelievers are no concern of ours. There are not just two, nor even three witnesses in whom every word stands[33] that Christ said this, but four testimonials of the highest certainty and reliability: two from the circumcised and two from the uncircumcised,[34] so that both peoples could have their own legitimate authorities, either for salvation or for judgment. At all events He said the words, it

dixit ille qui dixit et facta sunt. Qui enim dixit in principio: *fiat lux*, et facta est lux de nihilo, non potuit, dicendo de pane: *hoc est corpus meum*, ita fieri efficere? Et qui tacita virtute aquam vertit in vinum, non efficatius poterat, si quid tamen "efficatius" de deo dici debet, sonante vocaliter eadem virtute vinum ipsum in sanguinem suum transferre? Quod si quis apud se dicat potuisse hoc facere unum illum hominem, qui etiam deus erat, ceteris vero, qui hoc non sint, impossibile esse, nos quoque cum eo sentimus, sic tamen, ut per ministerium humanum Christum ipsum operari fateamur. Dixerat enim cum adhuc esset cum hominibus mortalis: *sine me nihil potestis facere*, et inmortalis effectus, cum caelos ascensurus esset corporaliter: *ecce ego*, inquit, *vobiscum sum omnibus diebus usque ad consummationem seculi*. Quia enim ex duabus diversis naturis, altera circumscripta, altera incircumscripta, conpersonatus erat, per circumscriptam de loco ad locum transmigrabat, per incircumscriptam vero, qua inlocaliter ubique est totus, cum eis remanebat, nec tamen filium dei a filio hominis separabat. Denique et priusquam filius hominis actu ascenderet in caelum, cum filio dei ibi erat, ipso attestante ubi ait: *et nemo ascendit in caelum, nisi qui descendit de caelo, filius hominis qui est in caelo*. Si ergo ibi erat per unitatem personae, quo nondum ascenderat per proprietatem naturae, propter eandem unitatem caelum ascendens cum hominibus in terra remanebat. Quis enim alius dicebat: *Saule, Saule, quid me persequeris?* Neque enim putandus est angelus ei pro Christo apparuisse, cum ipse Saulus, effectus postea Paulus, dicat: *novissime omnium tanquam abortivo visus est et mihi*, et alio loco: *nonne dominum Iesum Christum vidi?*

Aut vero Saulus adhuc infidelis raptus est in caelum ut illic ei Christus loqueretur, aut ipse Christus descendit e caelo, quod semel tantum fieri oportet *in voce archangeli et in tuba dei*, quando *omnes qui in monumentis sunt audient vocem filii dei et procedent*. Ipse igitur cum hominibus manens et homines baptizat per homines et consecrat quicquid per homines consecratur. Utrumque enim in evangelio habemus, et quod Iesus baptizaret, et quod non ipse baptizaret, sed discipuli eius. Baptizat nimirum, quia quando corpus sub quibusdam verbis sollemnibus in aqua mersatur, ipse animam mortuam, peccata remittendo, vivificat, sicut in evangelio loquitur: *venit hora, et nunc est, quando mortui audient vocem filii dei et qui audierint vivent*, quod non nisi de resurrectione animarum accipi potest. Baptizat et homo, per cuius manus et linguam opus illud administratur; sed maxime ac principaliter ille baptizat, qui vim et efficientiam totam prestat, propter quod

was Him that said them, and they came about.[35] For how could He who said at the beginning, *Let there be light*,[36] and the light emerged out of nothing, say of bread, *This is my body*, without it being so? And He who with silent power turned water into wine,[37] would He not better be able (if indeed "better" may be said of God) by the same power spoken out loud, to translate the same wine into His own blood? Supposing someone said to himself that that one man who was indeed God had been able to do this, but that it would be impossible for others who are not God. We would agree with that person: let us acknowledge nevertheless that Christ Himself can bring it about through a purely human action. Indeed, while Christ was still a mortal among humans,[38] He had said, *Without me, you can do nothing*.[39] And after He became immortal, when His body was about to ascend into heaven, He said, *Behold, I am with you always, to the end of the age*.[40] Since He had united in His person two natures (the one well defined, the other vague), He could move in His visible form from one place to another, but His invisible form is not bound to one place, but is everywhere, and so stayed with them: nor yet did he separate the Son of God from the Son of Man. Finally, before the Son of Man did in fact ascend into heaven, He was there with the Son of God, as He himself testified: *No one has ascended into heaven except the one who descended from heaven, the Son of Man, who is in heaven*.[41] Since He, as a unified person, was there when He had not yet ascended there because of His own nature, He could also, because of the same unity, ascend to heaven and yet stay with men here on earth. For who else said: *Saul, Saul, why do you persecute me?*[42] Do not think that an angel appeared in Christ's place to Saul, who was later named Paul, to make him later say: *Last of all, He appeared to me as to a child born at the wrong time*.[43] And in another place, *Did I not see our Lord Jesus Christ?*[44]

Either the hitherto unbelieving Saul was taken up into heaven,[45] so that Christ could speak with him there, or Christ descended from heaven, which will only happen once *with the voice of the archangel and the clarion call of the Lord*,[46] *when all those who are in their graves will hear the voice of the Son of God and come forth*.[47] He remains among men,[48] and baptizes them through other men, and consecrates what is consecrated by them. In the Gospel we find both: because Jesus used to baptize, and His disciples, not He, used to baptize as well. It is certain that He baptizes, since He revives the dead soul with its sins forgiven, when certain solemn words are spoken and the body is immersed in water, as it is said in the Gospel: *The hour comes, and it is now, that the dead will hear the voice of the son of God, and those who hear it shall live*,[49] which we can only say about the resurrection of the soul. So, too, does every man baptize whose mouth and hands perform this task: but in the first instance He baptizes who has all power and efficacy. On account of which, this was said by John the Baptist: *He above whom*

dictum est Iohanni Baptistae: *super quem videris Spiritum descendentem et manentem super eum, hic est qui baptizat.* Alioquin baptismus unus non esset, sed, prout meritum hominis se haberet, alius dignior, alius indignior fieret, et quem homo sanctior baptizaret, ille melius baptizatus esset. Sed absit, quia quicumque baptizat in nomine Patris et Filii et Spiritus sancti, dignus an indignus, sanctus aut peccator, catholicus aut hereticus, nihil interest, quoniam ministerium tantummodo illorum est, nec ab eis sed per eos, si recte loqui volumus, baptizatur. Christus igitur per manum et os sacerdotis baptizat, Christus per manum et os sacerdotis corpus suum et sanguinem creat. *An experimentum queritis eius, qui in me loquitur Christus?* Dicebat hoc quidem apostolus non arroganter se efferendo, sed veraciter docendo Christum in ministris suis et loqui quod ipsi loqui audiuntur et operari quae ipsi facere videntur, propter quod sacerdos est in aeternum, quia ipse est qui baptizat et qui immolat. Nam quod semel fecit passibiliter per semetipsum, id cottidie agit inpassibiliter per eos, quibus potestatem dedit filios dei fieri. Nec aliter melius posse intellegi puto quod apostolus de illo ait: *qui est ad dexteram dei, qui etiam interpellat pro nobis*, quam ut interpellatio ista fiat non verba proferendo, sed obedientiam atque humanitatem suam per conmemorationem passionis deo patri conmendando. Hoc quoque in eiusdem sacramenti institutione, cum iam sub articulo ipsius passionis agonizaret et ad dolores carnis mox futuros prescio spiritu pavitaret, hoc, inquam, certissimum pignus sui dilectis discipulis relinquens, *hoc facite*, inquit, *in meam conmemorationem*, conmemorationem caritatis erga vos, pro quibus animam meam pono, et obedientiae apud patrem, quia *sicut mandatum dedit mihi pater, sic facio.*

Quod si quos movet cur hoc sacramentum non visibiliter transmutetur in speciem carnis et sanguinis, attendant hoc quod apostolus ait: *per fidem*, inquit, *ambulamus et non per speciem*. Est autem fides, sicut ipse diffinit, *sperandarum substantia rerum, argumentum non apparentum*. Si enim id, quod intus sunt, sacramenta foris ostenderent, fides, ex qua iustus vivit, non solum otiosa, verum nulla omnino esset: *quod* enim *videt quis, quid sperat*? Ut ergo fides exerceatur credendo quod non apparet, vitale sacramentum sub specie corporea, ut anima in corpore, utiliter latet. Denique et baptismus aqua quaelibet oculis intuentium et non intellegentium videtur, et homo baptizatus quid aliud quam quod erat antea apparet? Non enim ex nigro albus aut ex inlitterato grammaticus per lavacrum regenerationis efficitur. O animalis

you see the Spirit descending and remaining, he is the one who baptizes.[50] Otherwise there would not be one baptism: on the contrary, it would depend on the merit of the man, one more fit would do it, another more unfit would do it; and a man baptized by the holier man would be better baptized. God forbid! Whoever baptizes in the name of the Father, and of the Son, and of the Holy Ghost, be he worthy or unworthy, holy or sinful, Catholic or heretic, it does not matter; since their function is limited, it is not by them, but through them (to use precise terms) that baptism occurs. Therefore, it is Christ who baptizes through the hand and mouth of the priest, and it is Christ who creates His Body and Blood through the hand and mouth of the priest. *Do you seek experience of Him who speaks in me, Christ?*[51] Indeed the Apostle was saying this not arrogantly to exalt himself, but truthfully, to teach that it is Christ who, in His ministers, both says what they themselves are heard saying and does what they themselves are seen doing; on account of which He is the priest for all eternity,[52] since He is the one who baptizes[53] and who sacrifices. Since what He did once through Himself, when He was liable to suffering, He now does daily without that liability, through those whom He has granted the power to become sons of God.[54] I think what the Apostle says of this—*He sits at the right hand of God and intercedes for us*[55]—can be understood in no better way than that this intercession happens not by offering words, but by commending His obedience and His humanity to God the Father by reminding Him of the Passion. When He instituted this same sacrament, when He was already suffering just before the Passion itself, and was trembling at the bodily suffering which was soon at hand, as He knew beforehand, this was His most sure pledge which He left to his beloved disciples, when He said: *Do this in remembrance of me*;[56] in remembrance, that is, of the love I have for you, for whom I lay down my life, and also of my obedience to the Father, *for I do as the Father has commanded me.*[57]

Concerning the question that worries some, namely, why this sacrament does not mutate visibly into the species of flesh and blood, let them attend to what the Apostle says: *we walk by faith, not by sight.*[58] And faith is, as he defined it himself, *the assurance of things hoped for, the conviction of things not seen.*[59] Indeed, if the sacraments were to show on the outside that which is inside, faith, by which the righteous man lives, would become not only useless but nothing at all:[60] for *what does a man see when he has hope?*[61] So, for faith to operate and believe what cannot be seen, the sacrament of life is hidden under the substance of the species, in human fashion like the soul in the body. Lastly, not only is the water of any baptism seen by the eyes of those who are present, but also the baptized man, what else does he appear than what he was before? Indeed, the bath of regeneration does not produce white from black, nor a grammarian from an illiterate.[62] O animal-like humans

homo, qui non percipit ea quae dei sunt, o caro, carnalibus phantasiis magis quam vino ebria, quousque ab his tam infeliciter ludificaberis? Non enim similis est hic error denegationis salutis animarum aut illusionibus somniorum aut de aquis et speculis resultantium imaginationum, quia ibi sine periculo fallitur, hic cum detrimento, inrecuperabili nisi resipiscatur, erratur.

Expergiscere ergo et clama: *infelix ego homo! Quis me liberabit de corpore mortis huius?* Et respondebit tibi consolatio apostolica: *gratia dei per Iesum Christum dominum nostrum.* Quod et si credimus verum esse, non liberabit hominem, non solum a molestia spiritalis pugnae quam hoc in loco "mortem" appellat, sed nec a miseria errorum, nisi gratia dei per Iesum Christum dominum nostrum. Melius tamen id intellegimus si humanae naturae concretionem et vim, quae nimirum in sensu corporis et animi intellectu tota constat, diligenter inspiciamus et quid per utrumque quid ve per alterutrum valeat breviter perstringamus. Sunt namque multa quae solo sensu corporis agimus, sicut videre atque audire; pleraque, sicut scribere et legere, quae communiter sensus cum intellectu administrat; plurima vero, ad quae sensui nullus prorsus accessus esse potest, sicut ad rationem numerorum, ad proportiones sonorum, et omnino ad notiones rerum incorporearum, quae omnia non quilibet intellectus, sed purus atque etiam usu limatus percipere meretur. Nec me fugit illa prima, quae duas istas potentias precedit, sed ad hoc nostrum institutum nihil visa est attinere, et curandum est ne longiore quam oportet utamur digressione. Conamur enim adiuvante divina gratia ostendere quod nulla humana facultas, quae plane et ipsa est divina largitas, nequaquam tamen sufficiens sit, quamlibet se extendat, ad conprehendendam altitudinem sacramentorum, quibus initiamur et perficimur ad aeternam salutem quae est in Christo Iesu domino nostro. Proponamus itaque baptismum ipsum, et quid ibi sensus, quid ratio deprehendat videamus. Liquorem esse aliquem tactus interrogatus pronuntiat; visus, si forte in vase est, quisnam liquor sit addubitat; sed gustus, tanquam tertius testis adhibitus, aquam esse incunctanter explorat. Ulterius, nisi fallor, hac in re officium suum sensus non pollicetur, at ratio longe longeque penetrat interius naturamque insensibilem perspicaciter intuetur, hoc est mobilem atque obtunsam esse, humidam substantialiter, frigidam naturaliter, in aerem sive in terram converti eam possibile esse, et siquid adhuc aliud, quod novimus aut ignoramus, de natura aquarum indagari potest. Quomodo autem per aquam et Spiritum anima regeneretur peccatorumque remissio tribuatur, sicut sensus carnis paulo ante docebatur non posse ad rationis excellentiam ascendere, ita profecto et minus forsitan valet

who do not perceive what is godly![63] O flesh, overcome even more by your own fancies than by wine, how long will you be so unhappily deceived by these things? This error of denying the salvation of souls is not like the illusions of our dreams or fancies reflected in water or mirror, since there we are deceived without any danger, but here we err with irrecoverable damage, unless we repent it.

So wake up[64] and call out: *Wretch that I am! Who will rescue me from this body of death?*[65] And the consolation of the Apostle will be: *Thanks be to God through Jesus Christ our Lord!*[66] Because if we believe it is true that humankind will only be liberated, not only from the burden of the spiritual struggle (which in this place he calls death), but also from the wretchedness of error, by the grace of God through Jesus Christ our Lord, we understand it better if we are willing to examine closely the makeup and essence of human nature, which consists without doubt of the bodily senses and the understanding of the mind, and then briefly assess what can be done by both, and what by one or the other.[67] For there is much that we do only through our bodily senses, such as hearing and seeing. But there is more, such as writing and reading, that the senses and the intellect do together. But to most things the senses have no access at all, such as the computation of numbers, the proportions of music, and generally knowing the incorporeal entities, all of which any intellect which is clear and, to be sure, refined by practice, is entitled to perceive. Now I do not overlook the first faculty mentioned, which surpasses the other two, but it did not seem relevant to our subject, and we should beware of digressing at greater length than is appropriate. Indeed, with the aid of divine grace, we can try to show that no human faculty (and we owe them all to divine generosity) is sufficient (however extensive it may be) to comprehend the loftiness of the sacraments,[68] in which we are initiated and which we perform for our eternal salvation, which is in Jesus Christ our Lord. Let us therefore take that baptism and see what our senses make of it, and what our minds grasp. Upon investigation by touch, it is obvious that there is some kind of liquid. To the eyes, when it is poured into a vase, it is unclear what kind of liquid it is. But taste, as a third test, immediately indicates it to be water. Beyond that, if I am not mistaken, the function of the senses can offer nothing more in this matter. But our mind penetrates far deeper.[69] It clearly grasps its insensible nature: that is, that it is mobile and variable, a wet substance, cool by nature, capable of being converted into gas and into a solid; and beyond that, everything that we know or do not know about the nature of water can be discovered. However, how the soul can be regenerated by water and Spirit, and forgiveness of sins be granted[70]—if our bodily senses have just been shown not to be capable of reaching the height of our minds, by the same token we can assert that our mind is assuredly not—and perhaps less—capable of comprehending

ratio ad hoc inscrutabile archanum aspirare, et tamen firmiter tenemus verissimeque confitemur animam incorpoream per aquam corpoream renasci atque in eum statum, quo fuerat Adam nondum prevaricator, reparari. Deum quoque ipsum, cuius enigma omnem superat intellectum, non solum novimus esse quod et infideles fatentur, verum etiam unum eundemque trium personarum incircumscriptum, ubique inlocaliter totum, neque tamen sensu aut ratione hoc habemus conprehensum. Unde ergo id percipimus? Et quid amplius quam animal rationale sumus? Hic prorsus evigila atque animadverte, preter sensum et rationem tercium quiddam prestantius, quo deum ipsum attingere possumus, nos habere, non innatum sed ex gratia dei conlatum, hoc vero esse fidem christianam. Quo bono nihil melius, nihil beatius in hac vita humano generi potuit provenire, quod ipse *mediator dei et hominum*, omnem naturam tam creatam quam creatricem in se ipso gerens, quando voluit et quibus voluit, non quibus debuit (alioquin gratia iam non esset gratia) prerogavit.

Hac duce nocturna, ut ait Tullius de Cinosura, fidenter atque inerranter dirigimur per mare huius seculi inportuosum et densissima errorum caligine undique circumfusum. Hic plane thesaurus ille est, quem a sapientibus et prudentibus abscondit et revelavit parvulis, et haec est illa gratia dei, qua se apostolus liberandum esse confidit per Iesum Christum dominum nostrum. Cuius quidem fidei quantas laudes quantaque preconia in epistola ad Hebreos exequatur, longum est occupatissimo et properanti ad calcem epistolae pertractare. Satis iam mihi videor, si forte et tibi videar, id quod tantopere moliebar assecutus esse, siquidem ut sacramenta christiana non sint humana ratione, cui impossibile est ea conprehendere, discutienda, sed fide, hoc est divino illo munere, immobiliter retinenda. Nam cum in baptismo nihil amplius quam aquam sensus et ratio deprehendat, fides introrsum descendens virtutem in eo vivificam perspicue atque simpliciter intuetur. Ideo autem dixi "simpliciter," quia nullo modo melius quam simpliciter fides custoditur. Odit enim dominus nimios scrutatores, quod in patre Iohannis Baptistae declaratur et in eo, qui baptismi mysterium curiosius investigans gravi repulsus elogio audivit: *tu es magister in Israel et haec ignoras?*

Sed scatet semper humanus animus, et eorum maxime, qui per philosophiam et inanem quandam fallaciam magnum aliquid sibi esse videntur, gestiens rerum omnium causas et rationes enucleatim decerpere, quod tamen, sicut de creaturae statu atque habitu non est superfluum, ita prorsus de creatoris sensu atque consilio nimis est temerarium: *quis enim cognovit sensum*

this arcane secret. We nonetheless hold firmly, and very rightly admit, that the immaterial soul is reborn through material water, and returns to the state Adam was in before he sinned. God Himself, whose mystery exceeds all understanding,[71] we know to be not only what even the infidels acknowledge, but also to be one and at the same time the unseparated total of three persons, and we understand this with neither our bodies nor our minds. Then how do we know this? What are we more than a rational animal?[72] Here give your full attention to this consideration: besides senses and a mind, we possess a third something of more value with which we can reach toward God Himself, which is not innate but provided through the grace of God, and this is Christian faith. In this life, nothing better for humankind, or more holy, could derive from this good thing, which *the mediator between God and men*[73] has Himself given in advance, having within Him all nature both created and creative, whenever He wanted and to whomever He wanted, not to whom He owed it (for otherwise grace would not be a gift).

This our nocturnal guide,[74] as Cicero calls the Pole Star, will lead us faithfully and without fail through the endless sea of these times,[75] harborless and everywhere covered with a thick fog of error. Because this is truly the treasure that He kept hidden from wise and intelligent men and revealed to the least of men, and it is the grace of God, by which the faithful Apostle knew he was saved, through Jesus Christ our Lord. Indeed because he sets out such great praises and such great proclamations of his belief in the letter to the Hebrews,[76] it would take much time to investigate when you are busy and in a hurry to finish. But I imagine, and maybe you also, that we have more or less arrived at what I have been making such an effort to establish—always supposing that we should not discuss the Christian sacraments with the arguments of human reason, which cannot possibly comprehend them, but hold steadfast to them with this divine gift of faith. Indeed, while during a baptism our senses and our minds see nothing more significant than water, faith penetrates inward and beholds a life-giving power in it, simply and clearly. I say "simply," because there is no other way for faith to be preserved. The Lord dislikes overzealous inquirers, as is apparent from the Father John the Baptist,[77] and the one who tried fervently to discover the mystery of baptism and was brought to a halt by the firm reprimand: *You are a teacher in Israel, and yet you do not know these things?*[78]

But the minds of men are ever filled with something[79] (especially those who imagine, because of philosophy or some hollow fallacy, that it is a great something), longing to gather in the minutest detail the causes and reasons for everything. But just as this is necessary for the natures and habits of the creatures, it is assuredly too bold for the essence and the designs of the Creator: *for who knows the Lord's inten-*

domini? Attamen idem doctores pompatici auditores suos a sensibilibus ad intellegibilia magnopere avocare solent voluntque eos, auctoritate sua contentos, multa quae necdum intellegunt credere. Quanto igitur aequius est, nos terrigenas vermiculos caelesti magistro subici eique per omnia credulos esse, qui, tam falli quam fallere nescius quia veritas est, omnia quaecumque vult facit quia omnipotens est. Et revera, quid magnum est creatori panem in corpus suum invisibiliter convertere, quem cottidie in corpus nostrum invisibiliter facit transire? Unde enim caro, unde ossa et nervi nisi ex cibis variis, quibus vescimur, in id molis ac roboris surrexerunt? Unde vero sanguis atque humores caeteri, quibus corpora nostra perluuntur, nisi ex his quae potando haurimus? Quod cum nemo dubitet verum esse, nemo tamen quomodo fiat ullo sensu corporeo deprehendere valet. Ideo apostolus, propheticum testimonium sibi advocans, *iustus*, inquit, *ex fide vivit*, et ipse dominus, titubanti discipulo visu et tactu satisfaciens, ait: *quia vidisti me, credidisti: beati qui non viderunt et crediderunt*. Si ergo beati qui credunt, miseri sine dubio qui non credunt. Quod ne simus, credamus, frater, quicquid de salutaribus sacramentis animarum nostrarum medicus nobis ordinavit, qui, plagas illas a latronibus inpositas, quas sacerdos et levita sibi prorsus incurabiles preterierant, hic Samaritanus noster curare descendens, sacramenta ista velud antidota quaedam et cataplasmata preparavit, sine quibus vitam et salutem aeternam impossibile est nobis conferri, ut beatus pater Augustinus in libro baptismorum parvulorum ait: Optime, inquit, Punici christiani baptismum ipsum nihil aliud quam salutem et sacramentum corporis Christi nihil aliud quam vitam vocant. Unde, nisi ex antiqua, ut existimo, et apostolica traditione didicerunt, preter baptismum et participationem mensae dominicae non solum ad regnum dei, sed nec ad salutem et vitam aeternam posse quemquam hominum pervenire? Hoc doctor magnificentissimus. Quem nos pueri sequentes, licet non passibus aequis, eadem tamen via gradientes.

Credamus, corde et ore confiteamur, verum corpus Christi esse quod invisibili virtute Christi per visibile ministerium sacerdotis de pane materiali creatur. Credamus etiam omnes renatos ex aqua et Spiritu, hoc sumentes, ipsi Christo incorporari. Qualiter autem incorporentur etsi impossibile est ratione probari, ex usu tamen rerum domesticarum perfacile est credi. Si enim sal, piper sive aliud fermentum, massam quamlibet corripiens, ita eam vi propria penetrat ut in suum saporem totam convertat, cur incredibile videatur tanto hoc tamque efficaci sacramento totum hominem in melius

tions?[80] Nevertheless, big-time teachers are much given to leading their listeners away from what is open to the senses in the direction of what is open to the mind, and they want them to accept on faith, and on their authority, many things which they in no way understand. It is therefore much more fit for us, earthly little worms, to be subjected to our heavenly teacher and believe Him in everything—He is as incapable of being deceived as He is of deceiving, since He is the truth,[81] and does all that He wishes to do, since He is almighty. And indeed, how is it a great thing for our Creator to change bread invisibly into His Body, which He daily invisibly assimilates into our bodies? Where else do our muscles and bones and sinews come from, if they have not grown in our bodies as bulk and solidity from the variety of foods we consume? Where else do our blood and our other bodily fluids that fill up our bodies come from than from those we imbibe? Nobody could doubt this, even though nobody can perceive with any bodily sense how it happens. That is why the Apostle adduces the testimony of the Prophet and says, *The righteous man lives by faith,*[82] and the Lord Himself, when He convinced His own doubting disciple by means of sight and touch, said: *You have believed because you have seen me. Blessed are those who have not seen and yet have come to believe.*[83] So they who have faith are blessed; wretched, beyond a doubt, are those who do not have faith. To escape which, let us, brother, trust in whatever the physician of our souls has ordained concerning the salvific effect of the sacraments. He who came down to care for those wounds inflicted by robbers, wounds which the priest and the Levite passed over as absolutely incurable by them, our Samaritan, has prepared the sacraments just like so many remedies and plasters.[84] Without them it is impossible for eternal life and salvation to be brought to us, as our holy father Augustine says in his book about the ordinary baptized people: "The Christians in Carthage most correctly call their baptism nothing other than salvation, and the sacrament of the Body of Christ nothing other than life. Where, if not from ancient and apostolic tradition (as I think), did they learn that apart from baptism and participation at the table of the Lord a man can arrive neither at the kingdom of God nor at eternal life and salvation?"[85] This is what our most outstanding teacher tells us. We follow him like his pupils, maybe not in his footsteps,[86] but at least along the same road.

Let us believe with our hearts and profess with our voices[87] that the invisible power of Christ, effective through the visible ministration of the priest, creates from earthly bread the real Body of Christ Himself. Let us also believe that all who are reborn from the water and the Holy Ghost, when they consume this food, become part of Christ Himself. Now quite how they are thus incorporated in Christ, although it is not possible for reason to test, can be readily believed from everyday household practices. If salt, pepper, or any other condiment can seize upon some mass[88] and so penetrate it by their own power that they change the

permutari, nisi eum, qui *iuditium sibi manducat et bibit non diiudicans corpus et sanguinem domini?* Magnum vero, dicat apud se aliquis, si tamen multiplex est corpus Christi, magnum ac mirificum est quod credatur et in caelo inmortaliter regnare et in terra, variis corruptionibus obnoxium, mortaliter laborare: hoc quippe est beatum ac miserum idem simul esse! Ita plane est. Habemus enim utriusque rei firmissimum documentum. Nam cum apostolus de membris Christi, hoc est de fidelibus, loqueretur, *sicut*, inquit, *corpus unum est et membra habet multa, omnia autem membra corporis, cum sint multa, unum est corpus, sic et Christus.* Ecce quomodo corpus et caput unum facit, utrumque scilicet appellans. Qui forsitan est et ille vir, de quo alibi dicit: *donec omnes occurramus in virum perfectum.* Non ait "in viros perfectos," sed "in virum perfectum." Cuius viri caput est ipse qui natus ex Maria virgine mortuus est et resurrexit, membra vero omnes electi ab initio usque ad consummationem seculi. Et quemadmodum in capite corporis nostri sensus omnes ipsaque ratio versatur, in cetero tamen corpore solus tactus, membris singulis officia singula sortitis, invenitur, ita nimirum de ipso capite nostro apostolus: *in quo sunt*, ait, *omnes thesauri sapientiae et scientiae absconditi.* Et item: *in ipso*, inquit, *habitat omnis plenitudo divinitatis corporaliter.* Utque hanc similitudinem conprobaret, paulo ante premisit: *et ipse est caput corporis aecclesiae.*

De membris porro sic loquitur: *unicuique nostrum data est gratia secundum mensuram donationis Christi.* Idem quoque ipse, verum profecto membrum illius capitis, de semetipso dicit: *ut suppleam*, inquit, *ea quae desunt passionum Christi in carne mea*, passiones utique Christi ea, quae Paulus ipse patiebatur, vocans. Christus igitur patiebatur in Paulo, crucifigebatur in Petro, Petrus et Paulus in Christo conversabantur in caelo: *nostra*, inquit, *conversatio in caelis est.* Et alibi multo fiducialius: *qui convivificavit nos*, inquit, *et consedere fecit in caelestibus in Christo.* Mirum sane! Adhuc colaphizabatur ab angelo Satanae in terra, et tamen gloriatur se conresuscitatum consedere in caelestibus in Christo, sed propter illam unionem atque conpagem membrorum hoc dicit. Quam alibi evidentius conmemorans *si patitur*, inquit, *unum membrum, conpatiuntur et omnia membra, et si glorificatur unum membrum, congaudent omnia membra.* Hoc quoque ipse dominus in evangelio sepe facit. Cum enim dicit: *Ego sum vitis et vos palmites*, et: *Nisi granum frumenti cadens in terram mortuum fuerit, ipsum solum manet; si autem mortuum fuerit, multum fructum affert*, quid per has similitudines nisi eandem conpagem insinuat, qua se

whole to their own flavor, why can we not accept that all of a man can be changed into a better by so great and so effective a sacrament, except that man who, *not discerning the Body* and Blood of the Lord, *eats and drinks judgment against himself*?[89] Suppose a man said to himself, "It is a great thing, and a marvelous, if the Body of Christ is manifold, that it is thought both to reign in heaven, immortal, and to be afflicted, mortal, here on earth, and liable to different corruptions: since this is to be at once blessed and wretched." Such is plainly the case. We have the most solid evidence for both things. For when the Apostle spoke of the members of Christ[90]—that is, of the faithful—he said, *For just as the body is one and has many members, and all the members of the body, though many, are one body, so it is with Christ*.[91] And see how he makes the body and the head one, naming them both of course. This is without a doubt the person of whom Paul speaks elsewhere: *until all of us come to be a perfect full-grown man*.[92] He does not speak of "perfect men", but "a perfect man." Of this man the head is the one who was born of the Virgin Mary, who died and is reborn; the members are all of the chosen ones, from the beginning until the end of time. Well now, the way that in the heads of our bodies are all our senses and our minds, while the rest of the body only has the sense of touch, and the way every member has its proper function, that is the way the Apostle describes Him who is our head: *In Him all the treasures of wisdom and knowledge are hidden*.[93] And again: *For in Him all the fullness of the Godhead dwells bodily*.[94] And to confirm this comparison once again, he said a little earlier: *And He is the head of the body of the church*.[95]

Paul also mentions the members in turn: *To each one of us was grace given according to the measure of the gift of Christ*.[96] Also, he said the same about himself—certainly a true member of this head—*in my flesh let me complete what is lacking in Christ's afflictions*,[97] calling the suffering, at least, which Paul himself was experiencing the suffering of Christ. Therefore Christ also suffered in Paul, and was crucified in Peter. Peter and Paul dwell in heaven in Christ. *Our homeland*, says Paul, *is in the heavens*.[98] And elsewhere his faith is even more manifest: *He has restored us all to life and has given us a place in the heavens, in Christ*.[99] This is astonishing. Hitherto "he was being buffeted by Satan's angel on earth,"[100] and yet he congratulates himself on "being restored and reunited with Christ in heaven"[101]: but it is on account of that unity and as it were that fabric of the members[102] that he says this. He mentions it more clearly elsewhere: *If one member suffers, all suffer together with it; if one member is honored, all rejoice together with it*.[103] The Lord Himself often concurs in the Gospel. When He says: *I am the vine, you are the branches*,[104] or *Unless a grain of wheat falls into the earth and dies, it remains just a single grain; but if it dies, it bears much fruit*,[105] what else is He hinting at with these metaphors but that same fabric?—in which He has deigned with so much goodness of heart to gather all His

membris suis tanta benignitate dignatus est conferre, ut eis gloriam suam conferre et ipsorum vicissim iniurias in se transferre nullo discrimine voluerit, excepto quod sicut vitis et palmites, cum sint unum lignum, non tamen vitis a palmitibus quicquam accipit, sed ipsa palmitibus id unde fructificent inmittit, et multa grana frumenti, ex uno prodeuntia, quamvis idipsum sint omnia, debent tamen uni illi quod sunt tanquam principio suo, nihil autem ipsum illis? *Gratia*, inquit, *dei sum id quod sum*, quidam fructuosus palmes et granum fructiferum. Ita nihil ipse aliunde mutuatus quicquid in quolibet sanctorum boni est inspirando inmittit et adiuvando perficit.

Pertinere ad hoc etiam videtur visio illa Nabuchodonosor regis de lapide parvo, id est Christo, qui de monte sine manibus abscisus, id est absque semine humano generatus, crevit in montem magnum et totam terram implevit. De monte abscisus crevit in montem, quia corpus, quod de massa humani generis modicum assumpsit, accedente undique fidelium numero *in immensum* sese dilatans crescere usque in finem seculi, donec totam terram impleat, non desistit. Hoc igitur, iam in ipso capite plene perfecteque glorificatum, deinde in quibusdam membris, de quibus scriptum est: *multa corpora sanctorum qui dormierant surrexerunt*, bene beateque in caelo recumbunt; in aliis vero adhuc laborat, vitam quippe hanc mortalem agentibus, in corpore isto tanquam in carcere morantibus, gementibus, dissolvi et esse cum Christo cupientibus. Sunt preterea et alia eiusdem maximi et vere gygantei corporis membra (neque enim frustra de illo cantatur in psalmo: *exultavit ut gygas*), quae tametsi, exuta penitus omni labe corporea, feliciter gloriantur, adhuc tamen beatificata auctius, resuscitatis in fine coaptatisque denuo corporibus inmortaliter victuris, spem firmissimam prestolantur.

Et hanc forte diversitatem partium, quibus corpus hoc mirabile est consertum, intuebatur psalmista, eructans in spiritu verbum: *astitit*, inquit, *regina a dextris tuis in vestitu deaurato, circumdata varietate*. Quae est enim regina nisi sponsa regis illius, de quo protinus subinfertur: *et concupiscet rex decorem tuum, quoniam ipse est dominus deus tuus?* Ipse est rex, ipse est deus, ipse sponsus, ipse caput eius, haec porro est aecclesia ipsius, ancilla per naturam, sponsa vero et corpus effecta per gratiam, impleto sacramento quod a seculo promissum erat: *erunt duo in carne una*. Quae nimirum circumdata est varietate membrorum, aliorum regnantium atque epulantium, aliorum egrotantium, peregrinantium, in lacrimis seminantium redemptionemque corporis sui expectantium. Sed hoc non semper: alioquin nihil usquam miserabilius esset. Quam diu ergo et

members, in conformity with His wish to confer on them His own glory, and on the other hand transfer to Himself their injuries, with no difference except that vines and branches, for example, though they be one tree, yet the vine takes nothing from the branches, but rather supplies that whence they might be fruitful; and many grains of wheat, coming forth from one, although they are all that very one, yet owe what they are to that one, as it were to their origin, it meanwhile owing nothing to them. *By the grace of God*, Paul said, *I am what I am*,[106] a fruitful branch and a fertile grain. Thus deriving nothing Himself from anywhere, He supplies, by inspiring them, whatever is good in any of the saints without distinction, and finishes the good by cherishing it.

It seems the vision of king Nebuchadnezzar is also about the same subject.[107] He saw a small rock—that is, Christ—which loosened itself from a mountain without interference from human hand—the way that He was conceived without human seed—and became a huge rock that filled all the earth. That stone grew into a mountain after falling from a mountain, since the body, which admitted only a small part of all of humanity, by swelling *to immense proportions*[108] thanks to the number of faithful coming in from all sides, does not stop growing until the end of time and all the earth is filled. That body is already complete and perfectly glorified as regards the head; secondly as regards some of its members of whom it is written: *Many bodies of saints, who had fallen asleep, rose again*,[109] and now they repose, blessed, in heaven;[110] but the body still suffers as regards other members, namely, those who lead this mortal life, who wait like prisoners in this other body and sigh and yearn to depart and be with Christ.[111] And of that immense and truly gigantic body (the psalm rightly says: *like a giant he has risen*[112]), there are other members who, although they gladly rejoice, inwardly freed of all bodily stain, yet still in addition they await the most certain prospect, more greatly blessed, and having been raised up at the end of time with bodies put together again, of living forever.

Maybe it is this variety of members that wondrously make up the body to which the psalmist alludes as, in the spirit, he utters the words: *at your right hand stands the queen in a gilded dress, surrounded with variety*.[113] Who else is this queen but the bride of the king, of whom it is said immediately after: *And the king shall admire your beauty, for He is the Lord your God*? He is the king, He is God, He is the bridegroom, and He is her head: she in turn is His Church, His servant in the natural order, become in fact through grace His bride and His Body, fulfilling the mystery that had been predicted since the beginning of time: *They will be two in one flesh*.[114] And she is surrounded by the variety of her members, some successful and exultant, others suffering and in exile, sowing in tears[115] but hoping for the salvation of their body.[116] But this state of affairs does not last; a worse situation is unimaginable. So how long will it take, until when? For the present, it will be as

quousque? Interim dum rex in accubitu suo iacet, moram quidem faciens, sed plane venturus. Qui cum apparuerit, ipsius vita, tunc et illa apparebit cum ipso in gloria, tunc denique varietas ista penitus auferetur, cum absorpta morte in victoria totum hoc corpus beata inmortalitate vestietur membraque omnia, capiti suo configurata, proprio mutuoque decore unanimiter congaudebunt. Dominus quoque Iesus, tradito regno deo et patri evacuataque omni virtute et potestate, exhibebit sibi aecclesiam non habentem maculam neque rugam aut quicquam eiusmodi et erit *deus omnia in omnibus.*

Poterat hoc latius atque limatius pertractari, poterant exempla evangelica atque apostolica, in idipsum consonantia, cumulatissime advocari, sed et ex voluminibus orthodoxorum patrum multa testimoniorum turba, multos nimirum codices inpletura, ad medium deduci. Et fecissem quidem, si talium insueto ac tantum secularibus litteris armato opusculum hoc condidissem. Sed audivi iam pridem te illis valefecisse atque sacris lectionibus sedulo insudare, ut mirum atque etiam incredibile videatur tale quippiam abs te oriri potuisse, nisi quod aiunt, ut pace tua dixerim, te, novitatum captatorem, veteres accusare atque probatissimos scriptores artium exauctorare, adeo ut Priscianum, Donatum, Boetium prorsus contemnas multaque eorum dicta, quae eruditorum omnium usu comprobante ad nos usque demanarunt, opposita auctoritate tua evertere coneris. Quae res tametsi plena est audaciae pervicacis, utcumque tamen ferri tolerabilius valet, quoniam ad salutem aeternam nullum forte aut certe minimum discrimen habet. Quicquid autem est in quo fides periclitatur, quae nos ducit ad vitam, id omni animae volenti pie vivere in Christo Iesu cautissime est a se repellendum, in proximo, quantumvis coniunctissimo, acerrime inpugnandum severissimeque vindicandum, iuxta illud caelestis oraculi edictum: *si oculus tuus vel manus tua vel pes tuus scandalizat te, erue, abscide et proice abs te.* Proinde cum audirem sepe iuvenes quosdam, qui ad nos descenderant, in claustris suis a prelatis eorum regulariter pulsatos esse eo, quod in lectionibus aecclesiasticis accentus tuos insolenter usurparent auresque fratrum aliter imbutas inusitatis quorundam verborum prolationibus offenderent, pro nihilo ducebam. Hoc autem genus plasphemiae nullo modo supersedendum putavi, primo ut deviantem proximum corrigere temptarem, deinde ne, ut sunt homines ad detrahendum precipites, ego errori illi affinis esse ipso silentio existimarer. Hortor itaque fraternitatem tuam in domino, si vitam diligis, quod indubitanter facis, si videre vis dies bonos, coerceas cor tuum et linguam tuam ab hoc malo et agas pae-

long as the king takes His ease,[117] deferring things certainly, but He must come. And when He does come, His beloved, she too will appear together with Him in glory.[118] Then at last she will be wholly divested of that diversity, the entire body (because death has been swallowed up in victory[119]) will be clothed in blissful immortality, and all its members, moulded with their head, will rejoice at their own and at each other's glory. Then the Lord Jesus Christ will deliver the kingdom to God the Father, destroying every power and every rule,[120] and He will present the Church to Himself without spot or wrinkle or any such thing,[121] and God will be *all in all*.[122]

This could be more extensively and meticulously examined. More than enough examples from the Gospels and the Acts of the Apostles could be cited to the same effect, and also from the writings of our orthodox forefathers could be brought to the purpose a multitude of proofs sufficient doubtless to fill up many books. I would certainly have done so if I had been writing this small treatise to one unaccustomed to such things and furnished only with secular writings. But I have long been hearing that you have said goodbye to the secular books and are sweating hard over sacred readings, though it seems a marvel, indeed incredible, that any such thing could have begun with you, except that the story (by your good leave) is that you, in hot pursuit of the new, are impeaching our old writers in the arts and showing the door to the best of them, so that you now despise Priscianus, Donatus, and Boethius and try to refute by your authority many of their statements which have come down to us, and which all scholars enthusiastically adopt.

Although this is a matter of stubborn audacity, it could be accepted one way or another, since it makes no or at least very little difference with regard to our eternal salvation. But whatever it is that puts faith at risk, faith that leads us to life,[123] it should be most warily pushed away (if our whole mind desires to live piously in Jesus Christ[124]) most bitterly opposed and most severely punished, in your nearest and dearest, however close, when put alongside that edict of the heavenly oracle: *If your eye or your hand or your foot offends you, cut it off and throw it away!*[125] Thus I used to think nothing of it when I frequently heard that youngsters who had visited us here [or who had been passed on to us] were regularly driven by their seniors so far that in their Church readings they immoderately adopted your tone and offended the ears of the brothers, which they filled, contrary to expectation, with unfamiliar propositions. However, I thought this sort of blasphemy should by no means be ignored, firstly so that I might try to correct the next one who strayed, and secondly—so quick are men to disparage—lest I be thought to share in that same error. I urge you, therefore, as a brother in the Lord, if you love life, which you indubitably do, if you wish to see better days, keep your heart and your tongue away from this evil and repent.[126] If you know that this corruption has touched your

nitentiam, si nosti hac peste percussam esse conscientiam, nec te deterreat pudor hominum, sed potius compellat illius terror, qui ait: *qui scandalizaverit unum de pusillis istis qui credunt in me, expedit ei ut suspendatur mola asinaria in collo eius et dimergatur in profundum maris.* Si enim sic iudicatur qui unum scandalizat, quanto dignus est supplicio qui aecclesiam totam conturbat? Nec tamen ille desperet: absit enim ut ulla moles, quantumvis ingens, humanae pravitatis obstruere posse putetur fontem divinae bonitatis, quoniam etsi peccatum habundat, sed superhabundat gratia.

Epistolam eandem, sed paulo largiorem, ecce iam secundo tibi mitto, quoniam properante legato priore propositam questionem de tripertita corporis Christi distinctione commode expedire copia non fuit. Credo etiam in manus tuas nondum illam pervenisse, nam si pervenisset nequaquam tam diu silentium tenuisses, maxime obsecratus a me per viscera misericordiae dei nostri, quod et nunc itero, ut quantotius rescriberes et evelleres ab animo meo scrupulum diu anxieque insidentem.

Et pax dei, quae exuperat omnem sensum, custodiat cor tuum et intellegentiam tuam in pace catholica quiescentem, quam quisquis non amat, nec amet nec ametur ab ullo, nisi resipiscat.

conscience, then the scorn of men should not deter you, but rather you should tremble with fear of Him who said: *but whoever offends one of these little ones who believe in me, it would be better for him if a great millstone were hung around his neck and he were thrown into the depth of the sea.*[127] If such a punishment is visited on him who offends only one, imagine the punishment that awaits him who offends the entire Church. But still that one must not despair: it is unthinkable that any weight of human evil, however heavy, could block divine benevolence, since even though sin abounds, still grace overmatches it.[128]

I send you now the same letter for the second time, somewhat more extensive, since in the first, which I wrote all too hastily, I did not have the opportunity to develop properly the question at hand of the three parts of the Body of Christ. I suspect that the first letter was not delivered to you, because if it had been, you would never have remained silent so long in the face of my earnest entreaty in the bowels of our God's compassion,[129] which I now repeat, to answer me as soon as possible and remove this burden that has been weighing for so long upon my heart and has caused me much concern.[130]

May the peace of God, which surpasses all understanding, guard your heart and your thoughts[131] in Catholic peace, for he who does not love this peace can neither give nor receive love, unless he repents.

Idem Beringarius in purgatoria epistola contra Almannum

Quod dicis audisse te quia dixerim non esse verum Christi corpus et sanguinem, vel panem et vinum altaris non esse a consecratione verum Christi corpus et sanguinem, noveris me nunquam manichaeorum admisisse sententiam. Illi enim fantasticum, ego verum et humanum corpus Christi fuisse et tenui et teneo. Ego Christi corpus, post expertam obedienter mortem, in immortalitatem et impassibilitatem sublimatum, ad dexteram Patris residere non nescio. Ego certissimum video, cum concedam dare aliqua ut Christi corpus fiat, concedendum mihi esse omnino, cum Christus nonnisi verum corpus habuerit, ut etiam verum corpus Christi fiat. Concedo autem panem et vinum altaris post consecrationem, secundum scripturas, Christi fieri corpus et sanguinem. Ac per hoc non concedere nullus possum post consecrationem ipsum panem et vinum facta esse fidei et intellectui verum Christi corpus et sanguinem.

Corpus ergo Christi et sanguinem, res dico ipsas sacramentorum mensae dominicae, non ipsa sacramenta, nusquam scripturarum appellatas inveni, nusquam appellavi figuram, similitudinem. Sacramenta autem ipsa, sicut sacramenta, ita etiam signa, figuram, similitudenem pignusque appellari, utrum de praesumptionis meae opinione afferam, ipse dijudica: Habes enim in X° de civitate dei ita sacramentum interpretatum a beato Augustino ut dicat: Sacramentum, id est sacrum signum. Diffinitionem signi habes eodem auctore in libro de doctrina christiana: Signum est res, praeter speciem quam ingerit sensibus, ex se faciens aliud aliquid in cogitationem venire. Non ait: In manum, in os, in dentem, in ventrem, sed: In cogitationem.

Item, quod etiam similitudo sit omne sacramentum eundem auctorem habes in epistola ad Bonefacium episcopum, ubi ait: Si sacramenta rerum quarum sacramenta sunt similitudinem non haberent, omnino sacramenta non essent. De figura habes eodem auctore in titulo psalmi tertii, ubi ait loquens de Juda: Cum adhibuit ad convivium in quo discipulis figuram corporis et sanguinis sui commendavit et tradidit.

Eodem modo beatus Ambrosius in libro de sacramentis: Sicut, ait, similitudinem mortis sumpsisti, ita similitudinem preciosi sanguinis bibis. In eodem: Fac, inquit, oblationem hanc ratam, rationabilem, quod est figura corporis et sanguinis Domini nostri.

Letter from Berengar to Adelmann[1]

When you say you have heard that I have said that the Body and Blood of Christ are not real, or that the bread and wine on the altar do not become the true Body and Blood of Christ through consecration, you must know that I have never shared the opinion of the Manichaeans. For they maintain that the Body of Christ is a phantasm, while I maintained and still maintain that the Body of Christ is real and human. I also know full well that the Body of Christ, after obediently suffering death and being raised to immortality and invulnerability, is seated at the right hand of the Father. I consider it to be absolutely certain that, once I in any way concede that Christ's Body does appear, I frankly have to admit that since Christ only had a real Body, only the real Body of Christ appears. Now I do agree that the bread and wine on the altar become Christ's Body and Blood after the consecration, in accordance with the authorities. And thus I cannot possibly disagree that after consecration the bread and wine have become, to the faith and to the intellect, the true Body and Blood of Christ.

I call the Body and Blood of Christ the *res sacramenti* of the divine meal, not the sacraments themselves; and never have I found them referred to in the authorities as figures or semblances, and never have I called them so myself. But judge for yourself whether or not I allege that the sacraments themselves as such are to be called "signs," "figures," "semblances," or "substitutes," out of a conceit based on my own authority: you can find the sacrament interpreted thus in the tenth book of *De civitate Dei* by St. Augustine, where he states: "A sacrament is a sacred sign."[2] The definition of a sign from the same authority can be found in the book *De doctrina Christiana*: "A sign is a *res* which of itself makes some other thing come to mind, besides the impression that it presents to the senses."[3] He does not say, "to the hands, the mouth, the teeth, and the belly," but: "to the mind."[4]

That each sacrament is also a likeness can also be found in the letter by the same author to Bishop Boniface, in which he notes: "If the sacraments did not have a resemblance to the *res* for which they are sacraments, then they would not be sacraments at all."[5] On the word "figure," you have the same author under the heading of psalm 3, where he says, speaking of Judas: "And then he invited him to the meal during which he entrusted to his disciples the figure of His Body and Blood."[6]

Similarly, St. Ambrose mentions in his book on the sacraments: "As you have consumed the likeness of His Body, so do you drink the likeness of the precious Blood."[7] And in the same text: "Make this offering as valid and reasonable, since it is the figure of the Body and Blood of our Lord."[8]

Possem, si res in infinitum non abeat, quanta velit quisque de scripturis subscribere. In scripturis enim Patrum, ad quas me scripto tuo mittebas, ad quas utinam satis ipse accessisses, luce publica eminet circa quid admittat mensa dominica figurae, pignoris, signi similitudinisque vocabulum, circa sacramenta videlicet, non res sacramentorum, cum constet nichilominus verum Christi corpus in ipsa mensa proponi, sed spiritualiter interiori homini, verum in ea Christi corpus ab his dumtaxat qui Christi membra sunt incorruptum, inattaminatum inatritumque spiritualiter manducari. Hoc Patres publice praeconantur, aliudque esse corpus et sanguinem, aliud corporis et sanguinis sacramenta non tacent; et utrumque a piis, visibiliter sacramentum, rem sacramenti invisibiliter, accipi, ab impiis autem tantum sacramenta commendant, nichilominus tamen sacramenta, secundum quemdam modum, res ipsas esse quarum sacramenta sunt; universaque ratio, universa auctoritas exigit, si constat quod dixerit aliquis: Hic panis est meum corpus, vel: *Panis quem frangimus* est Christi corpus, eum constituisse modis omnibus panis superesse, non absumptam esse substantiam.

Idem infra

Sicut michi constat vulgus et Paschasium, ineptum illum monachum Corbiensem, quam longissime dissentire ab Apostolo, Evangelista et autenticis majorum dictis, si moderatione christiana admiseris quae, propitia divinitate, scripturus sum, constabit et tibi, constabit etiam ipso auctore qui ait: *Qui erubuerit me et meos sermones, erubescam et ego eum coram Patre meo*. Ea est autem vulgi et Paschasii non sententia sed insania: in altari portiunculam carnis dominicae etiam nunc manibus frangi, etiam nunc hominis exterioris dentibus atteri. Contra ineptum istud ait Evangelista: *Accepit panem, benedixit panem, fregit panem, discipulis dedit panem, dicens: "Accipite panem. Hoc est, haec res, hic panis meum est corpus"*; et Apostolus ait: *Panis quem frangimus corpus Christi est*.

Idem infra

Adversarii ergo, vulgus, et cum vulgo insanientes Paschasius, Lanfrannus et quicumque alii ita causam intendebant: panem et vinum usque ad

I could continue to quote from the authorities as much as you could wish, but this would extend the matter into eternity. For in the writings of the Fathers, to which you referred me in your letter, without yourself having made sufficient reference to them, it is clearly apparent concerning what *res* the divine meal allows the terms "figure," "substitute," "sign," and "likeness": namely, concerning the sacraments, not concerning the *res sacramenti*. It is evident that the real Body of Christ is displayed on that table, but spiritually to the inner man, and that the real Body of Christ on it is spiritually consumed, at least by those who are members of Christ, and is consumed intact, unsullied, and undamaged. This is clearly professed by the Fathers, and they do not omit to say that the Body and Blood are one *res* and that the sacraments of Body and Blood are another. They recommend that the faithful accept both of these, the sacrament as visible, and the *res sacramenti* as invisible, while the heathen are recommended to partake only of the sacrament. Meanwhile the sacraments are no less, in one way or another, the *res* of which they are a sacrament.[9] All reason and all judgment demand that when it is agreed that someone has said: "This bread is my Body,"[10] or "The bread that we break is the Body of Christ,"[11] he has established that the bread still exists in every way and that the substance of it is not taken away.

Continued by the same

It is unquestionable to me that the common people and Paschasius, that foolish monk from Corbie, are as much in disagreement as possible with the Apostle, the Evangelist, and the authentic words of the ancients. This will be just as unquestionable to you if you accept with Christian moderation the things that, God willing, I shall write here: and they will also be unquestionable to the Teacher, who said: *Who is ashamed by me and my words, for him I shall also be ashamed before my Father.*[12] It is then not a belief but a folly of the rabble and of Paschasius, that on the altar of the Lord a bit of meat, of all things, is broken by human hands and forsooth chewed by human teeth. To such a fool the Evangelist replies: *He took bread, blessed the bread, broke the bread and gave the bread to his disciples saying: "Take this bread. This, this res, this bread, is my Body."*[13] And the Apostle says: *The bread we break is the Body of Christ.*[14]

Continued by the same

My opponents, then, the common herd, and with them the deluded Paschasius and Lanfranc, and whoever else, present the case as follows: the bread and the wine are

consecrationem constare in altari, urgente consecratione panem et vinum per corruptionem vel absumptionem sui in portiunculam carnis Christi sensualiter transire et sanguinis.

Mea vel potius scripturarum causa ita erat: panem et vinum mensae dominicae non sensualiter, sed intellectualiter, non per absumptionem, sed per assumptionem, non in portiunculam carnis, contra scripturas, sed, secundum scripturas, in totum converti Christi corpus et sanguinem. Hoc ego ratione, hoc secundum scripturas constantissima firmabam auctoritate:

Ratio, consulta intus veritate, quae menti humanae sola supereminet, renunciat in conversione rerum sensualium, id est per corruptionem sui seu absumptionem, qualis fuit virgae Moysi in serpentem, serpentis in virgam, molis corporeae uxoris Loth in statuam salis, aquae nuptialis in vinum omniumque ciborum ac potuum in carnem totius pene animalis et sanguinem, necessarium esse ante corruptionem alterius alterum non existere, corrupto nunc primum altero alterum nunc primum posse incipere; ac per hoc, si secundum hoc conversionis genus in altari res agitur, posse panem per corruptionem sui transire sensualiter sed in eam quae nunquam prius extiterit carnem; et quia Christi caro, sicut superius dictum est, per tot jam annos perfecta constans immortalitate, nunc primo ad corruptionem panis minime potest esse incipere, nichil in altari de carne Christi sensualiter haberi omnino necessarium esse.

Eadem ratio, sub judice veritatis, convincit verba Domini quibus enunciat: Hic panis est corpus meum, vel: Panis quem ego dedero caro mea est, ut hoc accipiamus sicut placet tibi; illa nichilominus apostoli Pauli ubi ait: *Panis quem frangimus* corpus Christi est, esse falsissima si quis mensae dominicae panem atque vinum non superesse contendit, cum negare non possis parte subruta (unde superiora satisfaciunt) totam etiam non posse constare.

Auctoritas non deerat evidens et copiosa, quamquam etiam hoc contiguum sit rationi, evangelica et apostolica. Evangelista enim et apostolus Paulus, sicut accepisse et benedixisse, ita etiam panem fregisse Dominum discipulisque dedisse, panem nichilominus discipulos ad jussum Domini accepisse et comedisse luce clarius indicant.

present on the altar until the consecration and, when the consecration acts upon them, the bread and wine change perceptibly into a piece of the flesh and the blood of Christ by dissolution or "absumption" within themselves.

My view, or rather that of the authorities, is as follows: that the bread and the wine from the Lord's table are not transmuted into a piece of flesh—which contradicts the authorities—but into the whole Body and Blood of Christ—which is in accordance with the authorities; and this change is not perceptible to the senses, but intellectual, and does not happen through "absumption" but through assumption. I have confirmed this position judiciously and in accordance with the authorities with the most dependable validity.

Reason, in inner discussion with truth (and only truth surpasses the human mind[15]), tells us that in alterations to perceptible *res* by internal dissolution or by absumption (examples are the staff of Moses, which changed into a snake and from a snake back into a staff; the body of Lot's wife, which turned into a pillar of salt; or the water that turned into wine at the wedding;[16] not to mention the transition from food and drink into the body and blood of almost all living beings)—reason tells us that of necessity before the dissolution of the one, the other does not exist, and that only after the one has suffered dissolution can the other first begin to come into being. And it follows, if this is the category of change that takes place on the altar, that bread can change perceptibly through internal dissolution, but only into flesh which was simply not there before. So the flesh of Christ, as mentioned above, unchanging for so many years in perfect immortality, can hardly now be brought into new existence upon the dissolution of bread: thus it is absolutely necessary that there be nothing perceptible upon the altar of the flesh of Christ.

Reason, checked by truth, proves to be utterly false the words of the Lord in which He announces, "This bread is my Body"[17] or, "The bread I give you is my flesh,"[18] whichever you prefer, and disproves no less the words of the Apostle Paul, when he says: "The bread we break is the Body of Christ,"[19] if we maintain that the bread and the wine from the Lord's table do not remain [after the consecration], since it would be impossible to deny that, once a part is destroyed (as was previously demonstrated) the whole cannot persist.

There has been no lack of copious and clear evangelical and apostolical statements, although this matter falls in the domain of reason. For the Evangelist and the Apostle Paul show with more than enough clarity that, just as it was bread that the Lord took and blessed, so it was bread that He broke and gave to his disciples, and it was no less bread that the disciples accepted and ate at the bidding of the Lord.

Idem infra

Beatus Augustinus distinctione prosequitur sacramentorum et rerem quarum sacramenta sunt, sicut in XXI° de civitate Dei, ubi ait: Ostendit quid sit non sacramentotenus, sed et revera Christi corpus manducare. Item in sermone quodam: Hujus rei sacramentum alicubi cotidie, alicubi certis intervallis temporum de mensa Domini sumitur, quibusdam ad vitam, quibusdam ad exitium, res vero ipsa omni homini ad vitam, nulli ad exitium. Item in Evangelio: Ac per hoc, qui non manet in Christo et in quo non manet Christus, proculdubio nec manducat ejus carnem, nec bibit ejus sanguinem, etiamsi tantae rei sacramentum in judicium sibi cotidie indifferenter accipiat. Item: Qui manducaverit ex hoc pane non morietur in aeternum, sed quod pertinet ad virtutem (id est rem) sacramenti, non quod pertinet ad visibile sacramentum. Sed nimis longum facio. Ad libros tantum qui volet accedat.

Interpretatur autem sacramentum beatus Augustinus in X° de civitate Dei ita: Sacramentum, id est sacrum signum. Vi autem verbi, quod est sacrare ad religionem pertinere notum est omnibus; et, noto dicendi genere, res in religione consecrata non solum res consecrata vel sacrosancta, sed dicitur etiam ipsa sacratio vel sacramentum, sicut egregius aliquis non solum justus, sed etiam ipsa justitia, non solum spiritualis vel caelestis, sed etiam caelum ac spiritus, contraque impius non solum carnalis vel terrenus, sed caro ac terra nominatur.

Multis autem in locis non ad hanc interpretationem ponitur sacramentum. *Sacramentum*, inquit Apostolus, *hoc magnum est: ego dico in Christo et in aecclesia*, ubi in verbo sacramenti accipitur allegoriae misterium.

Secundum superiorem interpretationem, diffinit beatus Augustinus sacramentum in quadam epistola: Sacramentum est invisibilis gratiae visibilis forma. In libro de catecizandis rudibus: Sacramentum est divinae rei invisibilis signaculum visibile. In libro de paenitentia: Sacramentum est divini misterii signaculum. In libro contra Faustum: Non sunt aliud quaeque sacramenta corporalia nisi quaedam quasi verba visibilia, sacrosancta quidem, sed tamen mutabilia et temporalia. Augustinus in libro de civitate Dei: Sacrificia visibilia signa sunt invisibilium, sicut verba sonantia signa sunt rerum.

Signum etiam idem beatus Augustinus diffinit in libro de doctrina christiana: Signum est res, praeter speciem quam ingerit sensibus, aliud aliquid ex se faciens in cogitationem venire.

Continued by the same

St. Augustine continues with the distinction between the sacraments and the *res* which the sacraments represent, as in book 21 of *De civitate Dei*, in which he says: "This shows what it is to eat Christ's body in reality, and not sacramentally."[20] Also, in one of his sermons: "The sacrament of this *res* is consumed from the Lord's table, in some places daily, in others at intervals, to some it brings life, to some death, but the *res* itself leads to life for every man, and to death for none."[21] Also on the Gospel: "And therefore, who does not reside in Christ and in whom Christ does not reside, will no doubt not eat his Body nor drink his Blood, even if he indiscriminately receives the *res sacramenti* every day, bringing judgment upon himself."[22] And further on: "Who shall eat this bread shall not die for all eternity, but this belongs to the power (that is, the *res*) of the sacrament, and not to the visible sacrament."[23] But I ramble on. Who wishes to know more must turn to the books.

Yet in the tenth book of *De civitate Dei*, St. Augustine explains "sacrament" as follows: "A sacrament is a sacred sign,"[24] and everyone knows what "consecrate," by the power of the word itself, means for religion. In common parlance a sacred *res* in religion does not only mean that sanctified or most holy *res*, but it also denotes the sanctification itself or the sacrament. By the same token, an excellent person is not only just but he is justice itself, not only spiritual and heavenly, but also heaven and spirit, and in contrast with this a godless man is not merely carnal and earthly, but is called "flesh" and "earth."

But in many places "sacrament" is not based on this definition. *This*, the Apostle says, *is a great sacrament, and I take it to mean Christ and the Church*,[25] whereby the word "sacrament" is understood as the mystery of allegory.

According to the above interpretation St. Augustine defines sacrament thus in one of his letters: "A sacrament is the visible form of invisible divine grace."[26] In the book *De catechizandis rudibus* he says: "A sacrament is the visible sign of the divine mystery."[27] In his book on penitence: "A sacrament is a sign of the divine mystery."[28] In the book against Faustus: "Sacraments that are experienced by the body are nothing other than a kind of visible words, most holy ones surely, but still variable and temporal."[29] In his *De civitate Dei* Augustine notes: "Sacrifices are visible signs of invisible things, as words are audible signs of things."[30]

What a sign is, Augustine also defines in his book *De doctrina Christiana*: "A sign is a *res* which of itself makes some other thing come to mind, besides the impression that it presents to the senses."[31]

Discutiendum erat revera ratiocinandumque ut hoc de sacramentis non opinione praesumeres sed ratione, vel in ipsa veritate vel in autenticarum scripturarum prosecutione; hisque anidmaversis, contra eos qui se quod manu tenent amississe quaeruntur, etiam circa hoc tali ratiocinatione consisteres:

Qui sacramenta corporis, sacramenta sanguinis dicere non refugitis, sacramenta autem signa esse scripturis contradicere non potestis, aliud sacramentum corporis, aliud corpus, aliud sacramentum sanguinis, aliud esse sanguinem necessario constituitis; mensaeque dominicae, cui vos putabatis deferre, pessime contraitis, dum in ea nichil esse nisi portiunculam carnis ac sanguinis, non de ratione, cui soli ad veritatem ipsam patet accessus, non de auctoritate, sed de insania vulgi, Paschasii atque Lanfranni vestrique cordis stupidissimi opinione proponitis, qui tamen in ea mensa Domini sacramentum corporis, sacramentum sanguinis in infinitum citare publice non desistitis.

Discussion and reasoning have indeed been necessary to make you accept this view on the sacraments, not based on prejudice, but based on reasonable conviction, founded either on truth itself or on the acceptance of authentic texts. Now, considering this, you can stand firm on this subject, against those who complain of having lost what they are holding in their hands, with reasoning such as this:

"Those of you who do not hesitate to celebrate the sacraments of the Body and the sacraments of the Blood cannot contradict the written authorities who say the sacraments are signs. You further are obliged to agree that the sacrament of the Body is one thing and the Body itself is something else, and that the sacrament of the Blood is one thing and the Blood is something else. And you most sinfully act against the Lord's table, which you supposed you were honoring, in claiming that there is nothing present on the altar but a piece of flesh and some blood; claiming this not on the basis of reason, which alone has access to this truth, and not on the basis of any authority, but on the basis of the delusions of the people, and of Paschasius and Lanfranc, and on the basis of the fancies of your own extremely dull minds. Yet you persist in openly and endlessly proclaiming the sacrament of the Body and the sacrament of the Blood on that table of the Lord."

Epistula Adelmanni ad Hermannum

Nobilissimae sedis archiepiscopo nobiliori H[ermanno], A[delmannus] inquilinus civis Spirensis urbiculae summam felicitatis aeternae.

  Novi quosdam vestri ordinis, et quidem satis probatos satisque eruditos, qui quoties in aecclesiis suis populo dei triticum spiritale distribuunt, expletis omnibus, quae ad fructum sanctae aedificationis pertinere intelligunt, manus sursum levare et peccata sua confiteri iubent; quo facto confestim absolutionem et remissionem eorum omnium illis tribuunt tanta facilitate, quanta forsitan de pecunia propria obolos tres nollent cuiquam relaxare. Hoc itaque audientes nonnulli fratrum, qui ex divino munere aliquantam sacrae scripturae facultatem habent et tamen propter reverentiam sacri ordinis obloqui nihil audent, vehementer scandalizantur, scientes rem prorsus illicitam fieri, quae nulla sanctorum patrum auctoritate defendi possit et ad internitionem imperitae multitudinis laqueus diabolicus sit, existimantis se nec confessione postea nec paenitentia indigere, sed omnia crimina sua tamquam denuo baptizatis dimissa sibi esse, acceptaque hac mortifera securitate nec pericula animarum suarum metuunt et iterare flagitia sua vel graviora eis addere pro nihilo ducunt, quippe quae iterum atque iterum tam facile ignoscenda sibi esse confidunt. Huc accedit quod ipsa ligandi solvendique auctoritas usu nimio pervulgata minus ponderis habere videtur et, ut fieri solet de omnibus rebus usitatis, apud mentes insipientium facile vilescit. Vides itaque, domine mi, quam late pateat hoc malum.

  Quod nefarium, quod plenum plasphemiae et omni modo illicitum esse evangelica tuba toto mundo intonante ostenditur. *Quis* enim *potest peccata dimittere nisi solus deus*? Cui nimirum omnis homo veraciter dicit: *Tibi soli peccavi*. Putant autem hanc potestatem se accepisse in eo quod dixit dominus discipulis suis: *quaecumque ligaveritis super terram, erunt ligata et in caelis, et quaecumque solveritis super terram, erunt soluta et in caelis*. Sed hoc sancti doctores nostri ad officium dispensationis, non ad ius potestatis pertinere volunt, dicentes tantam esse oportere cum deo concordiam sacerdotis, ut quod ante tribunal divini examinis de actibus humanis invisibiliter decernitur, hoc ipse velud quidam mortalis deus apud homines visibili quadam specie exsequatur. Dictos quippe deos esse sacerdotes quisquis sacras litteras scrutatur non ignorat, sed et ista aecclesia terrestris beatae illius civitatis imaginem quandam gerit, ut quisquis ab illa ob inmanitatem alicuius sceleris exulaverit, idem ab hac tamquam

Letter from Adelmann to Hermann

To the honorable Hermann, archbishop of a considerable city, Adelmann, resident of the town of Speyer,[1] wishes supreme eternal bliss.

It has come to my attention that each time certain members of your clergy—who are nevertheless sufficiently experienced and educated—distribute the bread to the Lord's people in their churches, they, after completing all those things which they understand to serve the interests of their Church, instruct the people to raise their hands and confess their sins. When this is done, they immediately grant them forgiveness and absolution for all their sins, as easily as if they were giving someone no more than three oboles from their purse. Some brothers who hear this and who possess in their divine profession some competence in matters of Scripture, but who dare not speak out against this practice out of respect for the cloth, are deeply shocked, knowing well that this business is indubitably illicit; it could not be condoned by any authority of the Church Fathers, and it would be a devilish snare for the downfall of the inexperienced masses, who believe that they need no further confession or atonement, but that all their crimes are forgiven as they are for the newly baptized. Once this deadly conviction has been established, they no longer fear danger for their souls, and they think nothing of repeating their shameful acts or even adding worse ones to them, since they trust that these will always be forgiven them with equal ease. Added to this, the power itself to condemn or absolve will become commonplace through such frequent use, and will appear to lose its worth. It will easily become worthless in the minds of fools, as usually happens with commonplace things. You see, my Lord, how significant this business is.

That it is criminal, that it is blasphemous and in every way unacceptable, is announced by the Gospel clarion, sounding to the entire world: *Who but God alone can forgive sins?*[2] To Him all men unquestionably say truly, *Against You alone have I trespassed.*[3] They think they have already received this power because of what the Lord said to his disciples: *whatever you bind on earth will be bound in heaven, and whatever you loose on earth will be loosed in heaven.*[4] But our saintly scholars believe that this appertains to the profession of dispensation and not to the *ius potestatis*.[5] They say that the like-mindedness of the priest and God must be so great that what is invisibly decided in the court of divine investigation into human conduct, the priest will, almost like a mortal god on earth, accomplish in a sort of visible version for the people.[6] All who peruse the Scriptures know full well that these mortal gods are priests. But even this earthly Church bears a certain resemblance to the holy city, so that someone who is banished from that city for the heinousness of a crime is also isolated outside the walls of this Church like

leprosus extra castra separandus sit, cumque per modum legitimae satisfactionis illuc rediisse videbitur, tunc per sacerdotale ministerium quasi mundatus huic redintegratur. Denique sacerdotes testamenti veteris non mundabant leprosos, sed mundatos in templum inducebant. Qua ergo temeritate sacerdotes novi testamenti lepram spiritalem mundare se profitentur? Quem umquam sanctorum inveniunt cuiquam peccatori dixisse: ego dimitto tibi peccata tua ac non potius communicatis ieiuniis et orationibus id eis, quibus subvenire volebant, a domino impetrasse? Quod legimus in Aecclesiastica Historia fecisse Iohannem apostolum pro iuvene illo, quem a latrocinio revocatum Christo iterum parturiebat. Sed et ipse *Filius hominis*, habens *potestatem in terra dimittendi peccata*, devitata personae suae expressione non ait: remitto tibi omnia peccata tua, sed quasi verecunde: *homo*, inquit, *dimittuntur tibi peccata tua*. Noverat plane paraliticum illum longo atque acerbissimo dolore purgatum indulgentiam mereri, sicut et illum, quem XXX et octo annos in infirmitate habentem in probatica piscina evangelio testante curavit. Et audent filii hominum aliena peccata ignota atque indiscussa dimittere, quorum neque ipsi conscii sunt neque paenitentiae testes existunt? Nonne hoc est quod de fallacibus prophetis per prophetam suum dominus conqueritur, dicens: *mortificant animas quae non moriuntur et vivificant animas quae non vivunt?* Quo vero ordine potestas ista administrari debeat, per prophetam alium evidenter pronuntiat: *probatorem*, inquit, *dedi te in populo meo robustum et scies et probabis vias eorum*. Probandi sunt quippe gressus singulorum, qualiter incesserint per viam morum, et antequam proferatur humanum iudicium quorsum vergat divina sententia vigilanter est intuendum. Denique Lazarus prius est clamante domino vivificatus et postea a discipulis solutus, quem si ante vocem domini solvissent, ille nihilominus insensibilis foetidusque iaceret. Ita nempe exanimis anima prius excitetur evocante domino ab inferis peccatorum et sic absolvatur ministerio sacerdotum. Quisquis aliter agit, certum est nihil illum alii prodesse, sibi vero plurimum obesse, quia, sicut ait beatus Gregorius, ipsa ligandi et solvendi potestate se privat, qui hanc pro suis voluntatibus et non pro subiectorum meritis exercet. Considerandum vero est iuxta normam sanctorum patrum quae culpa precesserit, quae satisfactio sit secuta, habitaque sagaci discretione tum demum timide atque humiliter potestas officii est adhibenda, nec ita dicendum: dimittat tibi dominus peccata tua, et ego tibi dimitto, nisi forte familiaris sit iniuria quae sacerdoti ipsi a reo fuerit illata. De tali utique peccato fidenter dicere potest: indulgeat tibi dominus, et ego. Sed quemadmodum nemo ita iustus, nemo ita sanctus est ut dicere ipse

a leper.[7] And if satisfaction has been had and authorized, he can return, and will be restored here, purged, as it were, by the ministrations of priests. Finally, the priests of the Old Testament did not purify lepers but led them into the temple after they had been purified.[8] How bold are the priests of the New Testament to claim they can cure spiritual leprosy? Which saint can they find who has ever said to a sinner: "I forgive you your sins," instead of trying to obtain this from the Lord for those whom they tried to help, after they had fasted and prayed? We read in ecclesiastical history that the Apostle John did this for the young man for whom he was anxious when he was called back to Christ after his freebooting.[9] Even the *Son of Man* Himself, *who did have the power to forgive sins on earth*,[10] avoided speaking in His own name and did not say, "I forgive you all your sins," but, with a certain humility, *Your sins are forgiven*.[11] He clearly knew that the cripple who was cleansed by long-lasting and grievous pain deserved mercy,[12] just as the ill man who lived for thirty-eight years by the Sheep Gate Pool was cured, according to the Gospel.[13] Do then mere men have the audacity to forgive the sins of others, without knowing them or discussing them, and of which they have neither knowledge nor evidence of any atonement? Is not this what the Lord, through the Prophet, deplores in false prophets when he says: *They kill immortal souls and souls that have no life they give life*.[14] He does clearly indicate according to which law this power must be executed, in the words of another prophet. He says: *I have made you an assayer and tester among my people, that you may know and assay their ways*.[15] Judgment is necessary for the actions of some, as to the manner in which they have started "the way of the world,"[16] and before human justice is consulted, it must be verified what the divine view is. Finally Lazarus was first brought to life by the call of the Lord, and only then released by the disciples.[17] Had they released him before the Lord's call, he would have lain there insensate and stinking. Likewise, the lifeless soul must first be awakened by the Lord's calling it forth from the underworld of sinners, to be liberated by the ministrations of priests when already in this state. For whoever acts differently, it is certain that he shall benefit no one else: on the contrary, he shall cause himself much damage, since "he robs himself of the power to condemn and absolve, if he abuses this power for his own wishes instead of for the well-being of his subjects,"[18] as St. Gregory said. Besides the rule of the Church Fathers, one must determine what guilt has preceded and what satisfaction has followed and then, utilizing the utmost discretion, only then is the power of the profession timidly and humbly to be executed. Nor can this be by saying, "May God forgive you your sins, and I forgive you," unless perhaps for an injustice which was personal and committed against the priest himself. Concerning such a sin he can confidently say, "May the Lord forgive you as I do." But as no one is so just and so holy that he dare say, "I

presumat: ego iustus sum, ego sum sanctus, sic et multo magis cavenda est haec blasphemia contra Spiritum sanctum cuius proprium opus est remissio peccatorum, ne quisquam homo homini dicere audeat: ego tibi peccata tua dimitto. Si enim hoc potest, potest consequenter et illud dicere: ego te iustifico et non de solo deo dicemus: *deus qui iustificas impium*, quod tam impium est corde cogitare quam sacrilegum ore proferre.

Quid igitur? Evacuamus auctoritatem apostolicam clavesque a domino collatas sacerdotibus eripere temptamus? Minime quidem. Quid ergo amplius iuris a ceteris habere eos dicimus? *Multum* quidem *per omnem modum. Primum, quia credita sunt* eis *eloquia dei* ad evangelizandum populo dei, deinde, quod solis est concessum peccata hominum in hoc mundo diiudicare, congruam pro expiandis poenitentiam imponere ipsamque pro habitu atque affectu paenitentis arbitrio proprio temperare, exemplo videlicet evangelici illius villici, qui vocatis singulis debitoribus domini sui unicuique eorum de summa pecuniae quantum sibi videbatur, domino ipso approbante, remisit. Quid plura? Per corpus et sanguinem Christi, quod solis conficere licet aecclesiae visceribus, lapsos redintegrant, regnum caelorum, hoc est presentem aecclesiam, per potestatem a deo datam hominibus claudunt atque aperiunt. Sunt enim plerique seculares probabilioris vitae perfectiorisque scientiae quam ulli in sacris gradibus constituti, qui et missam celebrare et evangelium legere ceteraque huiusmodi optime administrare norunt, sed quia potestatem non acceperunt, facere hoc nullo modo presumunt. Hanc potestatem convocatis Iesus XII apostolis dedit et ab ipsis usque ad nos, immo etiam *usque ad consummationem seculi*, dignis indignisque sacerdotibus, sed ipsam semper integram incorruptamque perseverantem, transire precepit. Ideo quisquis eam habet ministrum se eius, non possessorem esse existimare debet, *rationem vilicationis* suae summo patrifamilias in fine redditurus. Poterant autem qui eiusmodi sunt et hanc calumniam facile devitare et caetera omnia multo simplicius agere, si venerabilium doctorum, quorum sermones fructuosos cottidie audiunt, imitari vellent exempla. Illi enim, cum ad verbi divini tractationem se expediebant, primo omnium attentionem audientium blanda et benivola allocutione preformabant, deinde ingressi evangelicam sive apostolicam seu etiam propheticam explanationem pro captu popularis intelligentiae mysticorum sensuum caliginem dilucidare studebant atque inter omnia terrorem incutere peccatori, per confessionem vero et paenitentiam veniam polliceri, iustum ad melius exhortari, tum de instabilitate rerum presentium, de brevitate atque incertitudine huius vitae, de

am just, I am just, I am holy," so one must heed even more the blasphemy against the Holy Spirit,[19] whose exclusive part it is to forgive sins, and no man can say to another, "I forgive you your sins." If he can do this, he could as easily say, "I justify you," and then it will not be of God alone that we can say, *God, You who justify the unbeliever*[20]—which it is as impious to think in the heart as it is to speak the sacrilege aloud.

What then? Shall we annul apostolic authority altogether, and try to take away the keys that have been entrusted by God to the priesthood? Not at all. What power then have they more than others? *Much power and in every way. First, they are entrusted by God with authorized statements*[21] they are to spread among God's people; also, they alone are permitted to pass judgment on the sins of people in this world, and to order a fitting punishment in atonement, and to adjust this at their own discretion according to the physical and emotional state of the penitent, following the example of the steward in the Gospel who called the debtors of his master to himself one by one and returned to each of them in turn the amount of money he deemed best, after approval by his lord.[22] And what else? Through the Body and Blood of Christ, which can only be had in the bosom of the Church, they can restore the fallen and open and shut the kingdom of heaven,[23] which is the present Church, by the power vested in them by God. For there are many laymen who lead a more decent life, and have greater knowledge, than some who are invested in the spiritual orders. These people could both perform a Mass and read from the Gospel, and are quite capable of performing such tasks: but since they have not been invested with such power, they do not accept this charge. This power was given by Christ to the twelve assembled apostles.[24] He told them that it must pass from them to us and *even to the end of time*,[25] to worthy and unworthy priests, but itself always unimpaired, without corruption and steadfast. So everyone who has this power must keep in mind that he is not its possessor, and that he will be finally *accountable for his stewardship*[26] to the ultimate proprietor. The people involved could have both easily avoided this fallacy and executed all other business much more simply, if they had followed the example of the venerable scholars whose instructive statements they can hear every day. For when they were getting ready to discuss the word of God, they first prepared the attention of their audience with an agreeable and kindly speech; when they subsequently began the evangelical or apostolic or even prophetic explanation, they endeavored, for the understanding[27] of the popular intelligence, to dispel the thick mist around mystical perception, and especially to instill fear into the sinner, but all the while promising absolution after confession and atonement, and to exhort the just to even better behavior, by speaking of the mutability of temporal things, or of the shortness and uncertainty of this life, or of the severity of the judgment to come, or finally about the inexpressible

futuri examinis severitate, postremo de ineffabili beatitudine sanctorum, de infelicissima damnatione impiorum. De his ac talibus catholici predicatores nostri alii latius et suavius, alii angustius atque austerius, prout singulis gratia divina largita est, sermones aecclesiasticos texuerunt. Has vero nescio quas novas absolutiones, quas verius dicimus publicas deceptiones, nec in litteris eorum reperimus nec fecisse eos credimus nisi uno illo die, quo communionem aecclesiasticam more antiquitus instituto poenitentibus reddebant.

Audacter hoc, sed fideliter et nullo modo arroganter et humi procumbens percutiensque pectus meum maiestati vestrae scribere presumpsi, sciens per auctoritatis vestrae falcem nascentem et adhuc latentem istam heresim posse levius resecari, quoniam omnis sententia apud multos tantum habet ponderis, quantum est persona proferens potentiae secularis, at vero prudentia vestra nequaquam ita sentit neque rationem pensat ex fortuna hominis, sed hominem metitur ex momento rationis.

Deus omnipotens augeat vobis facultatem intelligendi et exequendi suam voluntatem.

bliss of the saints and the most calamitous damnation of the impious. By doing these and similar things our Catholic preachers, some broadminded and soft-spoken, others narrower and stricter, depending on the divine grace accorded each of them, composed their ecclesiastical discourses. These—what are we to call them?—these so-called "new absolutions" (which we should more truthfully call "deception of the people") we neither find in their writings nor, we believe, did they practice them, except on that one occasion when, by a long-established usage, they restored the penitent to the Church.

Confidently but in good faith, and by no means insolently and in deep supplication and salutation,[28] I have taken it upon myself to write this to your grace, knowing that the sickle of your authority could more efficiently prune away this burgeoning but until recently occluded heresy. Most people accord any view only as much weight as the worldly importance of the person who proclaims it; but of course your foresight does not think in this way, nor does it weigh an argument against the personal fortune, but measures the man by the strength of his argument.

May almighty God magnify your capacity to understand His will and execute it.

Rhythmus alphabeticus e manuscripto glembacensi

Aulus Mannus: Mitto etiam tibi rhitmicos versiculos juxta ordinem alfabeti digestos, quos, ante annos aliquot, cum adhuc Leodii essem, me ad amicos quosdam meos, quorum plures ipse noveras, lamentabiliter recensente, compositos, reperri nuper et edidi.

Armonicæ facultatis aspirante gratia
Refero viros illustres, litterarum lumina,
Quos recenti recordatur mens dolore saucia.

Bestiali feritate mors acerba seviens,
In scolare efferata tanquam leo rugiens,
Passim dedit stragis diræ plus quam aer pestilens.

Carnotenæ decus urbis, memorande pontifex,
Te primum, pater Fulberte, dum te conor dicere,
Fugit sermo, cor liquescit, recrudescunt lacrimæ.

Deploranda singillatim multa quidem memini,
Utpote convictor senis, herens sepe lateri,
Aure bibens oris fontem aureum melliflui.

Eheu! Quanta dignitate moralis industriæ,
Quanta rerum gravitate, verborum dulcedine,
Explicabat altioris archana scientiæ!

Floruere, te fovente, Galliarum studia;
Tu divina, tu humana excolebas dogmata,
Nunquam passus obscurari virtutem desidia.

Gurges altus ut minores solvitur in alveos,
Utque magnus ex se multos fundit ignis radios,
Sic insignes propagasti per diversa plurimos:

Hildierum, quem Pupillam nuncupare soliti,

The Rhythmic Poem, from the Gembloux Manuscript

Aulus Mannus: I send to you also these rhythmic verses, which are arranged in alphabetical order and which I crudely composed some years ago, while I was still in Liège, for some of my friends, many of whom you have known. I rediscovered these verses recently, revised them, and committed them to paper.

Encouraged by the grace of the harmonic art I recall famous men, shining beacons of letters, so that the mind, pained by recent sorrow, will remember them.

With beastly violence bitter death rampaged wildly, huffing like a lion among the students, wreaking havoc all around, worse even than the breath of the plague.

You, Father Fulbert, a credit and memorable bishop to the city of Chartres, I cite first, and as I try to recall you, my voice breaks, my heart melts, and my tears well up.[1]

Nevertheless, I remember well the sad scenes, since, dining companion of an old man, I often hung by your side and caught with my ears the honey-sweet stream of knowledge that welled from the golden spring of your mouth.

Alas, with such dignity and moral resolve, with such sincerity and such soft-spokenness did he explain the inner workings of the higher science.

It was your doing that studying flourished in Gaul; you refined human and divine dogmas. And you never suffered talent to be obscured by idleness.

Like a deeper maelstrom that separates into several smaller currents and like a great fire that sends out many rays, you too multiplied your many marks of distinction in various ways:

Hildegerus, who is sometimes called "little" because he was small of stature, was

Quod pusillus esset, immo perspicacis animi;
Cæterorum princeps atque communiceps presuli,

Is magistrum referebat vultu, voce, moribus,
Ypocratis artem jungens Socratis sermonibus,
Nec minus Pytagoreis indulgebat fidibus.

Karitate Sigo noster plenus atque gratia,
Multa prebens ore, manu, advenis solatia,
Singularis organali regnabat in musica.

Lambertus Parisiacum, Engelbertus Genabum
Occupabant lectionum otio venalium,
Questum pube de Francorum captantes non modicum.

Martini quoque concivem, sed non equæ sobrium,
Dignum duco memoratu Rainaldum Turonicum,
Promptum lingua, stilo largum, valentem grammaticum.

Næc tua, Girarde gibbe, te fraudabo nenia:
Ligerim flavum revisens ab Jordane et Solima,
Occidisti propter Mosam sub Virduni menia,

O! et te dira peremit emulorum factio:
Postquam mensus es Europam perflagranti studio,
Scolas multas expilasti, Waltere Burgundio;

Proh! si nunquam revertisses ad fines Allobrogum,
Quanta nunc auctoritate decorares Latium,
Docens quidquid revexisti ab ortis Hesperidum!

Quis te tandem, sacer heros, satis sepe fleverit,
Cujus [h]os et multos plures officina protulit,
Quorum quisque præ se tulit, quod te usus fuerit?

Reginbaldus Agripinas, vir potens ingenio,

nevertheless possessed of a keen mind, surpassed all others, and became the bishop's counselor.[2]

He reproduced his teacher in his appearance, his voice, and his manners. He connected the teachings of Hippocrates to the conversations of Socrates and was also fond of the followers of Pythagoras.

Our Sigo, full of charity and grace, was clever with words, helpful to strangers, and an exceptionally talented organ player.[3]

Lambert captured Paris and Engelbert Orléans through the ease of their lectures-for-sale, taking so small profit from the youth of France.

I also mention as memorable Rainald of Tours, who was quick-witted and generous in style, and also a mighty grammarian. He was a citizen of the same place as Martinus, but not as solemn as him.[4]

And your lament also, Gerard Gilbert, I shall not omit: how you upon your return to the Loire from the Jordan and Sion, were murdered by the Maas, beneath the walls of Verdun.[5]

And you also, Walter of Burgundy, were robbed of life by that terrible scheming amongst your enemies, after you had scoured Europe, with your blazing zeal ever pillaging schools.[6]

Oh, would that you had never returned to the land of the Allobroges![7] You would be such an authoritative asset to Latium as a teacher of all you had brought back from the garden of the Hesperides.[8]

Who could have mourned you enough, divine Fulbert? You whose words and efforts trained many notabilities, that each in turn exhibited what he had learned from you.

Regimbald of Aachen, a man with a strong mind, impressed his barbaric audience

Barbaras aures Latino temperans eloquio,
Notus arces ad Romanas ab usque Occeano,

Situs est in urbe nostra, longus hospes, Leggia:
Legia, magnarum quondam artium nutricula,
Sub Wathone, subque ipso, cujus hæc sunt rithmica.

Tres michi, Camena, cives memora de pluribus:
Illum, procul quem extinctum transalpinis febribus,
Lugent artes, lugent urbes cum suis primatibus

Vix amissum quereremur, Odulfo superstite,
Alestanum, quanvis erat [sic] veteris scientiæ,
Sicut hi, quos erudivit, satis pollent hodie;

Xerampelinos ornatus cum paucis jugeribus
Presul durus denegarat: at tu, Metti profugus,
Multas illic opes nactus, Warine, es et conditus.

Ypogeis et antiquæ parentis in gremio
Dormientes, excitandi mane mundi ultimo,
Pace æterna perfruantur, te, Christe, propitio!

Zelo grandi cor accensus pro carorum funere
Adelmannus hæc deflebat in Nemeti[1] littore,
Suos ipse idem illic observans cotidie.

Respondit Beringerius: "Nascitur ridiculus mus." Finit Beringerius contra Adelmannum, quem yronice vocat Aulum Mannum.

---

[1] *sup. lin.* id est Spirae

with Latin eloquence. He was famous from the Ocean to the gates of Rome.

For a long time he was a guest here in our city of Liège—Liège, the cradle of the higher sciences under the auspices of Wazo and of him who wrote these verses.[9]

Muse, let me remember, out of so many, three more citizens. First him that succumbed to the transalpine fever so far from here. He is mourned by the universities and by the cities and their notables.

Further we mourn, with Odulfus as a witness, the recently departed Alestanus. Even though he belonged to the old school of science, and likewise those he educated, they remain influential to this day.[10]

A hard patron had refused purple [literally: the color of dead leaves] robes of office, but you, Warinus, moved to Metz where you found much wealth, and are buried.[11]

May all those who rest in the grave, in the embrace of their ancestral ground, waiting to be awakened upon the last dawn of the world, enjoy eternal peace in your grace, Christ.

With a heart ardent with special reverence for the passing of his loved ones, Adelmann lamented their deaths on the beach of Speyer[12] in Gaul, while daily contemplating his own end as well.

It is here that Berengar answers: "a ridiculous mouse is born."
So does Berengar finish [his letter] to Adelmann, to whom he ironically refers as "little pony."

Rhythmus alphabeticus e manuscripto hafniensi

Armonicæ facultatis aspirante gratia
Stat referre summos viros, litterarum lumina,
Quos recenti recordatur mens dolore saucia.

Bestiali feritate mors acerba seviens,
In scolares conjurata velut hostis pestilens,
Passim dedit diræ stragi, plus quam modo insolens.

Carnotenæ decus urbis, memorande pontifex,
Te primum, pater Fulberte, dum te conor dicere,
Sermo fugit, cor liquescit, recrudescunt lacrimæ.

Deploranda singillatim multa quidem memini,
Utpote convictor senis, herens sepe lateri,
Aure bibens oris fontem aureum melliflui.

Eheu! Quanta dignitate moralis industriæ,
Quanta rerum gravitate, verborum dulcedine,
Explicabat altioris archana scientiæ!

Floruere, te fovente, Galliarum studia;
Tu divina, tu humana excolebas dogmata;
Nunquam passus es urgeri virtutem penuria.

Gurges altus ut in amnes scinditur multifidos,
Ut in plures fundit ignis se minores radios,
Sic insignes propagasti per diversa plurimos:

Hildigerum, quem Pupillam nuncupare soliti,
Quod pusillus esset, immo perspicacis animi;
Caeterorum princeps atque communiceps presuli,

Is magistrum referebat vultu, voce, moribus,
Ypocratis artem jungens Socratis sermonibus,

The Rhythmic Poem, from the Copenhagen Manuscript

Encouraged by the grace of the harmonic art it is fitting to recall famous men, shining beacons of letters, so that the mind, pained by recent sorrow, will remember them.

With beastly violence bitter death rampaged, conspiring against the students like a plague-ridden foe, wreaking worrisome havoc all around, in a most arrogant way.

You, Father Fulbert, a credit and memorable bishop to the city of Chartres, I cite first, and as I try to recall you, my voice breaks, my heart melts, and my tears well up.

Nevertheless, I remember well the sad scenes, since, dining companion of an old man, I often hung by his side and caught with my ears the honey-sweet stream of knowledge that welled from the golden spring of his mouth.

Alas, with such dignity and moral resolve, with such sincerity and such soft-spokenness did he explain the inner workings of the higher science.

It was your doing that studying flourished in Gaul; you developed human and divine dogmas. And you never allowed talent to be oppressed by penury.

As a deeper maelstrom splits up into several smaller currents and a great fire spreads out in many rays, you too multiplied your many marks of distinction in various ways:

Hildegerus, who is sometimes called "little" because he was small of stature, was nevertheless possessed of a keen mind, surpassed all others, and became the bishop's counselor.

He reproduced his teacher in his appearance, his voice, and his manners. He connected the teachings of Hippocrates to the conversations of Socrates and was also

Nec minus Pytagoreis indulgebat fidibus.

Karitate litterarum plus quam ipsis preditum,
Te, Radulfe, nudum texit hospitale Genabum,
Te virtutes effecere ex ignoto splendidum.

Libet et vos meminisse, nodosi lucripetæ,
Engelberte cum Lamberto, qui de nido paupere
Late caput extulistis circa ora[s] Sequanæ;

Martini quoque concivem, Reinbaldum Turonicum,
Quem credebam post illius syderis occubitum
Inter cellas singularem regnare philosophum.

Nec tua, gibbe Gerarde, te fraudabo nenia:
Liggerin flavum revisens ab Jordane et Solima,
Occidisti propter Mosam sub Virduni menia.

O! et te discerpsit atrox Remulorum factio:
Postquam mensus es Europam, flagrans acri studio,
Multas artes compilasti, Gerberte Burgundio;

Proh! si nunquam revertisses fatale Vesontium,
Quanta nunc auctoritate decorares Latium,
Docens quicquid revexisti ab hortis Hesperidum!

Quis autem te, magne, satis persepe defleverit,
Cujus scola tot tyrones tam spectatos edidit,
Quorum quisque pre se tulit quod usus non habuit?

Reinbaldus Aggrippinas, vir prestanti ingenio,
Sævam Reni pubem frenans Latiari imperio,
Notus arces ad Romanas ab usque Patavio,

Situs est in urbe nostra, longus hospes, Legia:
Legia, magnarum quondam artium nutricula,

fond of the followers of Pythagoras.

Hospitable Orléans covered your nakedness, Radulphus, more as an amateur than as a practitioner of letters, and your good qualities made you, from a nobody, illustrious.[13]

I would also like to mention you cunning profiteers, Engelbert and Lambert, who came from a wretched nest and raised your heads up high on the banks of the Seine.

[I would like to mention] also a citizen of the same place as Martinus, Reinbald of Tours, whom I believed to be in seclusion, after the fall of Martin's star, in the cells of the philosophers.

And your lament also, Gerard Gilbert, I shall not omit: how you upon your return to the Loire from the Jordan and Sion, were murdered by the Maas, beneath the walls of Verdun.

And you also, Gerbertus of Burgundy, were robbed of life by that terrible scheming among the citizens of Rheims, after you had scoured Europe, blazing with zeal and accumulating much knowledge.

Oh, would that you had never returned to fatal Besançon! You would be such an authoritative asset to Latium as you taught all you had brought back from the gardens of the Hesperides.

Who shall have lamented you, oh great one, often enough? You, whose school sent out so many recruits with such prominence, each of them exhibiting that which was of no use.[14]

Reinbald of Aachen, who kept the turbulent youths of the Rhine in check under the rule of Latium, was known from Batavia to within the walls of Rome.

For a long time he was a guest here in our city of Liège. Liège, the cradle of the

Non sic, o! nunc, dominante virtuti pecunia.

Tres michi, Camena dives, memora de pluribus:
Illum,quem procul extinctum transalpinis febribus,
Lugent arces, lugent urbes cum viris illustribus;

Vix amissum quereremus, Odulfo superstite,
Alestanum, quamvis esset veteris scientiæ,
Sicut hi, quos enutrivit, satis florent hodie;

Xerampelinos ornatus cum paucis jugeribus
Presul durus denegarat: at tu, Mettis profugus,
Multas illic opes nactus, Gerarde, es et conditus.

Yppogei[s] sub antique clausi matris gremio
Omnes uno funerati dormiunt quinquennio:
Pace æterna perfruantur, te, Christe, propitio!

Zelo vestri cor accensus, numeris funebribus
Adelmannus vos perornat his exequialibus,
Ter quaternos, quaternis minus uno versibus.

higher sciences! Alas, this is no longer so, since money rules over virtue!

Rich muse, Camena, let me remember, out of so many, three more persons. First him who succumbed to the transalpine fever so far from here. Strongholds and cities and their notables mourn him.

Further we mourn, with Odulfus as a witness, the recently departed Alestanus. Even though he belonged to the old school of science, and likewise those he nurtured, they flourish to this day.

A hard patron had refused purple robes of office, but you, Gerardus, moved to Metz where you successfully acquired and amassed great wealth and lie buried.[15]

They all sleep in the underworld, enclosed as before in the mother's womb, all buried during a period of only five years. May they enjoy eternal peace in your grace, Christ.

With a heart ardent with special reverence for you, Adelmann bedecks you with these obsequies in funereal verses, you three times four, in six times four minus one verses.

Notes

On Adelmann's Letter to Berengar

1. That is, Fulbert of Chartres.
2. After Lactantius, *De opificio Dei* 3 (CSEL 27:13$^{19-20}$).
3. Cf. Num. 21:22.
4. Cf. Ps. 140:9; Eccl. 9:3.
5. Ps. 139:6.
6. Ps. 118:165.
7. Ps. 118:32.
8. Cf. prayer on Holy Friday: *Oremus et pro haereticis et schismaticis.*
9. *Pax catholica* is an Augustinian expression (see *Enarr. in Ps.* 66.6; CCSL 39:864; *De baptismo* 1.2.3 (CSEL 51:147$^{20-1}$), 2.1.1 (174^{2}), 2.3.4 (179^{2}), and 3.17.22 (214$^{11-12}$).
10. Ps. 13:3.
11. Cf. Ps. 118:59.
12. Cf. 1 Cor. 11:22.
13. Cf. Apoc. 12:6.
14. Cf. Pseudo-Augustine, *Ad heremitas*, 7–8.
15. Cf. Zech. 8:19.
16. Cf. Acts 16:20.
17. "Old enemy" is Gregory the Great's expression for the devil; see *Homiliae in evangelia* 27.2 (CCSL 141:230^{25}) and 29.3 (247^{64}).
18. Cf. Is. 45:16.
19. Cf. Prov. 10:7.
20. Ps. 115:11.
21. Cf. Acts 17:24; 1 Jn. 2:15.
22. Cf. Cicero, *Lucullus* (ed. O. Plasberg [Leipzig: Teubner, 1922]), 89$^{6-12}$.
23. Ibid., 62$^{9-10}$. See also Augustine, *Contra Iulianum opus imperfectum* 4.103 (PL 45:1398): "Dixeras nos absurdius aliquid dicere quam qui nivem nigram esse dicebat."
24. Rom. 1:22.
25. Bar. 3:27.
26. Cf. Bar. 3:27.
27. Cf. Dan. 3:87; Matt. 5:3.
28. Matt. 11:25 (cf. Luke 10:21).
29. Jn. 14:6.
30. Cf. Apoc. 5:1 (for the contrast *intus-foris*) and 2 Cor. 7:5 (*foris pugnae, intus timores*).
31. Jn. 6:51–52.

32. Canon of the Mass, 7: "Qui pridie ..."
33. Cf. Deut. 19:15 (Matt. 18:16 and 2 Cor. 13:1).
34. Cf. Rom 4:9–12.
35. Cf. Ps. 32:9; 148:5.
36. Gen. 1:3.
37. Cf. Jn. 2:1–11.
38. Cf. 2 Thess. 2:5.
39. Jn. 15:5.
40. Matt. 28:20.
41. Jn. 3:13.
42. Acts 9:4.
43. 1 Cor. 15:8.
44. 1 Cor. 9:1.
45. Cf. 2 Cor. 12:2.
46. Cf. 1 Thess. 4:16.
47. Jn. 5:28–29.
48. Cf. Jn. 14:25.
49. Jn. 5:25.
50. Jn. 1:33.
51. 2 Cor. 13:3.
52. Cf. Ps. 109:4; Heb. 5:6 and 7:17 and 21.
53. Cf. Jn. 1:33.
54. Cf. Jn. 1:12.
55. Rom. 8:34.
56. Luke 22:19; 1 Cor. 11:24.
57. Jn. 14:31.
58. 2 Cor. 5:7.
59. Heb. 11:1.
60. Cf. James 2:20 and Augustine, *De diversis quaestionibus*, 76.1 (CCSL 44A:218³).
61. Rom. 8:24.
62. Cf. Tit. 3:5.
63. Cf. 1 Cor. 2:14.
64. Hab. 2:19.
65. Rom. 7:24–25.
66. Rom. 7:24–25.
67. Cf. Dan. 7:1.
68. Cf. Ambrose, *Epistula* 5 25.2 (CSEL 82:177²¹⁻²): "ut a me tamen sacramentis baptismatis initiaretur," and *De Abraham*, 1.9.84 (CSEL 32:556⁴⁻⁵): "nisi ... initiate sitis sacramento baptismatis." Also cf. Augustine, *Confessiones* 1.11.17 and 13.27.42 (CCSL 27:10¹² and 267²⁻³).
69. Cf. Cicero, *De finibus*, 2.21.68 (Bibliotheca Teubneriana 70:65)
70. Cf. Jn. 3:5.

71. 2 Cor. 10:5.
72. Cf. Quintilian, *Institutio oratoria* 5.10.56 (Bibliotheca Teubneriana 148:260).
73. 1 Tim. 2:5.
74. Cicero, *De natura deorum* 2.106 (Bibliotheca Teubneriana 72:91).
75. Sallust, *Iugurtha* 17.5 (Bibliotheca Teubneriana 152/1:68): "mare saevom inportuosum."
76. Cf. Hebr. 11:1–40.
77. Cf. Luke 1:18–20.
78. Jn. 3:10.
79. Cf. Plautus, *Persa* 2.1.9 (Budé 130:112): "scatet animus."
80. Rom. 11:34.
81. Cf. Ps. 113:3; 134:6.
82. Hab. 2:4 (Rom. 1:17; Heb. 10:38; Gal. 3:11).
83. Jn. 20:29.
84. Cf. Luke 10:30–34.
85. Augustine, *De peccatorum meritis et remissione* (CSEL 60:33[17–23]).
86. Cf. Virgil, *Aeneis* 2.724 (Bibliotheca Teubneriana, 186/1:61): "sequiturque patrem non passibus aequis."
87. Cf. Ps. 137:1.
88. Cf. 1 Cor. 5:6; Gal. 5:9.
89. 1 Cor. 11:29.
90. Cf. 1 Cor. 6:15.
91. 1 Cor. 12:12.
92. Eph. 4:13.
93. Col. 2:3.
94. Col. 2:9.
95. Col. 1:18.
96. Eph. 4:7.
97. Col. 1:24.
98. Phil. 3:20.
99. Eph. 2:5–6.
100. Cf. 2 Cor. 12:7.
101. Cf. Eph. 2:6.
102. Cf. Augustine, *Tractatus in Ioannem* 26.13 (CCSL 36:266[29–30]): "a compage membrorum."
103. 1 Cor. 12:26.
104. Jn. 15:5.
105. Jn. 12:24–25.
106. 1 Cor. 15:10.
107. Cf. Dan. 2:31–36.
108. 2 Cor. 10:13.15.
109. Matt. 27:52.

110. Cf. Matt. 8:11.
111. Cf. Phil. 1:23.
112. Ps. 18:6.
113. Ps. 44:10.
114. Gen. 2:24.
115. Cf. Ps. 125:5.
116. Cf. Rom. 8:23.
117. Cf. Song 1:11.
118. Cf. Col. 3:4.
119. Cf. 1 Cor. 15:54.
120. Cf. 1 Cor. 15:24.
121. Cf. Eph. 5:27.
122. 1 Cor. 15:28.
123. Cf. Matth. 7:14.
124. Cf. 2 Tim. 3:12.
125. Matt. 18:8–9.
126. Cf. 1 Petr. 3:10.
127. Matt. 18:6.
128. Cf. Rom. 5:20.
129. Cf. Luc. 1:78.
130. Cf. Cicero, *Pro Sexto Roscio* 2.6 (Budé 40/1,2:3): "ex animo scrupulum ... ut evellatis postulat."
131. Phil. 4:7.

On Berengar's Letter to Adelmann

1. The expression *Idem Beringerius* originates from the fact that in the Brussels manuscript, the letter to Adelmann follows Berengar's account of the Roman councils of All Saints 1078 and Lent 1079.
2. Augustine, *De civitate Dei* 10.5 (PL 41:282; CCSL 47:277).
3. Augustine, *De doctrina christiana* 2.1.1 (PL 34:35; CCSL 32:32).
4. Augustine, *Tractatus in Joannem* 26.6.12 (PL 35:1612; CCSL 36:266).
5. Augustine, *Epistola 98*, 9 (PL 33:364; CCSL 31A:233).
6. Augustine, *Enarratio in psalmum* 3.1 (PL 36:73; CCSL 38:8).
7. Ambrose, *De sacramentis* 4.4 (PL 16:443; CSEL 73:54).
8. Ambrose, *De sacramentis* 4.5 (PL 16:443; CSEL 73:55).
9. Cf. Augustine, *Epistola 98*, 9 (PL 33:364; CCSL 31A:233).
10. Cf. Matt. 26:26; Mark 14:22; Luke 22:19; 1 Cor. 11:24.
11. Cf. 1 Cor. 10:16.
12. Luke 9:26.
13. Matt. 26:26; Mark 14:22; Luke 22:19; 1 Cor. 11:24.
14. 1 Cor. 10:16.
15. Cf. Augustine, *De vera religione* 25.47 (PL 34:142; CCSL 32:217).
16. Cf. Ex. 7:10; Gen. 19:26; Jn. 2:1–12.
17. Cf. Matt. 26:26; Mark 14:22; Luke 22:19; 1 Cor. 11:24.
18. Cf. Jn. 6:51.
19. Cf. 1 Cor. 10:16.
20. Augustine, *De civitate Dei* 21.25.4 (PL 41:742; CCSL 48:795).
21. Augustine, *Tractatus in Joannem* 26.6.15 (PL 35:1614; CCSL 36:267).
22. Augustine, *Tractatus in Joannem* 26.6.18 (PL 35:1614; CCSL 36:268).
23. Augustine, *Tractatus in Joannem* 26.6.12 (PL 35:1612; CCSL 36:266).
24. Augustine, *De civitate Dei* 10.5 (PL 41:282; CCSL 47:277).
25. Eph. 5:32.
26. Augustine, *Epistola 105,12* (PL 33:401; CCSL 31B:57).
27. Augustine, *De catechizandis rudibus* 26.50 (PL 40:344).
28. Augustine, *Sermo 351: "De utilitate agendae poenitentiae"* 4.7 (PL 39:1543).
29. Augustine, *Contra Faustum* 19.16 (PL 42:356–7; CSEL 25:513).
30. Augustine, *De civitate Dei* 10.19 (PL 41:297; CSEL 47:293).
31. Augustine, *De doctrina christiana* 2.1.1 (PL 34:35; CCSL 32:30).

On Adelmann's Letter to Hermann

1. Cf. Sallust, *Catilina* 31.7 (Bibliotheca Teubneriana 152/1:25): " inquilinus civis urbis Romae."
2. Mark 2:7; Luke 5:21.
3. Ps. 50:6.
4. Matt. 18:18.
5. The *ius potestatis* is what would later be known as the *potestas clavium* (cf. Matt. 18:18). The Church based its institutional power upon this *potestas* from the eleventh century onwards. Together with the *correctio fraterna* (cf. Matt. 18:15–17), it served to ground the juridical power of the Church.
6. Cf. Ps. 81:6; Jn. 10:34–35.
7. Cf. Num. 5:2.
8. Cf. Lv. 14:11 and following.
9. Cf. Eusebius, *Historia ecclesiastica*, trans. Rufinus 3.23.6–19 (Eusebius, *Werke*, vol. 2.1, ed. Th. Mommsen [Leipzig: Hinrichs, 1903], 243^2 and 243^{27}).
10. Matt. 9:6; Mark 2:10; Luke 5:24.
11. Mark 2:5.
12. Cf. Mark 2:3-5.
13. Cf. John 5:2–9.
14. Ez. 13 19.
15. Jer. 6:27.
16. *Disticha Catonis*, ed. Carl von Reifitz (Saarbrücken: Verlag Classic Edition, 2010 [= reprint of the Basel edition of 1584]), 5: "in via morum."
17. Cf. Jn. 11:1–44.
18. Gregory the Great, *Homiliae in evangelia* 26.5 (CCSL 141:222^{106-08}): "Unde fit ut ipsa hac ligandi et solvendi potestate se privet, qui hanc pro suis voluntatibus et non pro subiectorum moribus exercet."
19. Cf. Mark 3:29.
20. Rom. 4:5.
21. Rom. 3:2.
22. Cf. Luke 16:1–8.
23. Cf. Matt. 23:13; Apoc. 3:7.
24. Cf. Matt. 10:1; Luke 9:1–2.
25. Matt. 28:20.
26. Luke 16:2.
27. Cf. Ambrose, *De Cain et Abel* 1.1 (CSEL 32:339^2: "pro captu nostro").
28. Cf. Luke 18:13.

On the Rhythmic Poem

1. In stanzas C, D, E, F, G, H, and Q Adelmann praises his famous teacher Fulbert of Chartres. He was born around 960 in Italy and died on April 10, 1028, at Chartres. In 1004 he became bishop of Chartres, where he had the cathedral built. During his tenure, the cathedral school developed into one of the most important centers of learning of its time. In the discussions between the dialecticians and the anti-dialecticians he chose the side of the second group, and emphasized keeping to tradition and the words of the Fathers. Divine mysteries remained invisible to all but the eyes of faith (see U. Mörschel, art. "Fulbert," in *Lexikon des Mittelalters*, 9 vols. (Munich and Zurich: Artemis & Winkler; Munich: LexMA, 1977–1998), 4:1014–15).
2. Stanzas H and I are about Hildegerus (Pupilla), who was one of Fulbert's favorite students. A philosopher, medical doctor, and musician, he was some kind of leading figure at the monastery of Saint-Hilaire-le-Grand at Poitiers. In this function, he returned to Chartres to become the chancellor of the cathedral and therefore also of the cathedral school. He died between 1028 and 1033.
3. Sigo was the deacon and cantor (he might even have been a composer himself) of the cathedral of Chartres. He was a student and later the trusted advisor of Fulbert. It is not known when he died.
4. Rainald was a philosopher, grammarian, and writer. As a writer he was perfect, but not as solemn as Martinus (of Tours). According to the Copenhagen version of the manuscript, Adelmann believed Rainald to be the only one adequately to represent philosophy at Chartres after Fulbert's death. He died sometime between 1028 and 1033. Also see Jules Alexandre Clerval, *Les écoles de Chartres au moyen âge du Ve au XVIe siècle* (Paris: Picard, 1895; reprinted, Geneva: Slatkine, 1977), 76–7.
5. This might be a reference to the master from Orléans who wrote the epitaph for Hugo, the son of King Robert (see Clerval, *Les écoles de Chartres*, 72–3).
6. There is nothing more known about this great traveler (see Clerval, *Les écoles de Chartres*, 83–4).
7. That is, the kingdom of Arles.
8. Stanzas O and P are devoted to Walter of Burgundy (he is called "Gerbertus" in the Copenhagen manuscript). Nothing else is known about him. It seems that he visited different schools throughout Europe and then returned to the Allobroges (or Besançon in the other version), where he fell victim to his enemies.
9. Wazo of Liège († 1048) was educated in the cathedral school of Liège at the time of Notker. In 1042 he was ordained bishop of Liège. In the struggle between worldly and spiritual power, he showed a clear preference for the second: no one must judge the pope. In his function as bishop, he strongly opposed simony.
10. Nothing is known about these men beyond what Adelmann recounts in these lines (see Clerval, *Les écoles de Chartres*, 88).
11. Warinus is called "Gerardus" in the Copenhagen manuscript. Nothing further is known about this person. He received a prebend, spent his life at Metz, where he became rich, and was buried.

12. Between the lines in the manuscript is written: "id est Spirae." The name *Nemeti* for Speyer stems from the Roman *Noviomagus Nemetum*.

13. It is unclear which Radulphus is referred to here. In all his nakedness he finds refuge in Orléans, where he rises to glory thanks to his virtues, that is, he is given a position of some prestige in the church of Orléans. In the records there is a mention of a Radulphus who was the deacon of the cathedral of Orléans, but there are other possibilities. Clerval thinks the reference is to a certain canon who was the economist of the cathedral of Sainte-Croix of Orléans (see Clerval, *Les écoles de Chartres*, 72).

14. These apparently senseless verses led Havet to conclude that the Gembloux manuscript represents a better lection (Havet, "Poème rythmique," 77).

15. The bishop of Liège, Durandus (1021–25), refused him a prebend so that he moved to Metz, where he was more successful (see Clerval, *Les écoles de Chartres*, 88).

Bibliography

Editions

(1) Letter from Adelmann to Berengar

Garetius, Johannes, *Johannis Garetii Lovaniensis de vera praesentia corporis Christi in sacramento Eucharistiae* (Antwerp: Martinus Nutius, 1561), esp. 67–8 [fragment].

"Divi Adelmanni ex scolastico Leodiensi, episcopi Brixiensis, De veritate corporis et sanguinis Domini in Eucharistia ad Berengarium, epistola," ed. Joannes Vlimmerius in his *De veritate corporis et sanguinis Domini Iesu Christi in Sacrosancto Eucharistiae sacramento* (Louvain: Hieronymus Wellaeus/Stephanus Valerius, 1651), 224–9.

"Adelmanni ex scholasctico Leodiensi, episcopi Brixiensis, De veritate corporis et sanguinis Domini in Eucharistia, ad Berengarium epistola," in *Maxima bibliotheca veterum patrum et antiquorum scriptorum ecclesiasticorum*, ed. Margarinus de la Bigne (Lyons: apud Anissonios, 1677), 18:438–440 [also in earlier editions of the *Bibliotheca patrum*].

"Adelmannus Berengario scribit," in *Annales ordinis Sancti Benedicti*, ed. Jean Mabillon, 6 vols. (Paris: Robustel, 1703–1739), 4:514–15 [fragments].

"De veritate corporis et sanguinis Domini in Eucharistia, ad Berengarium epistola," in *Veterum Brixiae episcoporum S. Philastrii et S. Gaudentii opera, nec non B. Ramperti, & Vener. Adelmanni opuscula*, ed. Paulus Galeardus (Brixen: ex typographia Joannis Mariae Rizzardi, 1738), 413–422. [This is the same edition as the one contained in: Paulus Galeardus, *Sancti Gaudentii Brixiae episcopi sermones qui exstant. Nunc primum ad fidem mss. codd. recogniti, et emendati. Accesserunt Ramperti, et Adelmanni venerabilium Brixiae episcoporum opuscula* (Padua: Josephus Cominus, 1720), 299–313.

Adelmanni Brixiae episcopi de veritate corporis et sanguinis domini ad Berengarium epistola, nunc primum e codice Guelpherbytano emendata et vltra tertiam partem suppleta, cum epistola Berengarii ad Adelmannum et variis scriptis ad Adelmannum pertinentibus, ed. Conrad Arnold Schmidt (Brunswick: Typis officinae librariae orphanotrophei, 1770), 1–33 [this book includes all of Adelmann's works].

Sudendorf, Hans, *Berengarius Turonensis, oder eine Sammlung ihn betreffender Briefe* (Hamburg: Perthes, 1850), 7–9.

"Adelmanni ex scholasctico Leodiensi episcopi Brixiensis De eucharistiae sacramento ad Berengarium epistola," in *Patrologiae cursus completus. Series latina*, ed. Jacques-Paul Migne, 221 vols. (Paris: Migne, 1844–1865), 143:1289–96 [text of *Maxima bibliotheca veterum patrum*].

"Adelmanni ex scholasctico Leodiensi episcopi Brixiensis De eucharistiae sacramento ad Berengarium epistola," in Raoul Heurtevent, *Durand de Troarn et les origines de l'hérésie bérengarienne*, Études de théologie historique 5 (Paris: Beauchesne, 1912), appendix 2, 287–303.

Huygens, Robert B. C., "Textes latins du XIe au XIIIe siècle," *Studi medievali. Serie terza* 8 (1967): 451–503, at 459–93 ["La lettre d'Adelman de Liège à Bérenger de Tours"].

"La lettre d'Adelman de Liège à Bérenger de Tours," in *Serta Mediaevalia. Textus varii saeculorum X–XIII in unum collecti*, ed. R. B. C. Huygens, CCCM 171 (Turnhout: Brepols, 2000), 166–201.

(2) Letter from Berengar to Adelmann

"Beringerius in purgatoria epistula contra Almannum," in *Thesaurus novus anecdotorum*, ed. Edmond Martène and Ursin Durand (Paris: F. Delaulne, H. Foucault, M. Clouzier, J.-G. Nyon, S. Ganeau, and N. Gosselin, 1717), vol. 4, 109–14.

"Lettre de Bérenger à Adelman de Liège," Appendix 2 in Jean de Montclos, *Lanfranc et Bérenger. La controverse eucharistique du XIe siècle*, Spicilegium sacrum Lovaniense. Études et documents 37 (Louvain: Peeters, 1971), 531–9.

(3) Letter from Adelmann to Hermann II of Cologne

"La lettre d'Adelman de Liège à Hermann II de Cologne," in *Serta mediaevalia. Textus varii saeculorum X–XIII in unum collecti,*, ed. R. B. C. Huygens, CCCM 171 (Turnhout: Brepols, 2000), 202–08.

(4) Rhythmic Poem

"Adelmanni scholastici Rythmi alphabetici de viris illustribus sui temopris," in *Vetera analecta sive collectio veterum aliquot operum et opusculorum omnis generis, carminum, epistolarum, diplomatum, epitaphiorum, etc.*, ed. Jean Mabillon, 2 vols. (Paris: Billaine, 1675–1676), 1:420–5.

Thesaurus novus anecdotorum, ed. Edmond Martène and Ursin Durand (Paris: F. Delaulne, H. Foucault, M. Clouzier, J.-G. Nyon, S. Ganeau, and N. Gosselin, 1717), vol. 4, pp. 113–14.

"Adelmanni scholastici rythmi alphabetici de viris illustribus sui temporis," in *Vetera analecta sive collectio veterum aliquot operum et opusculorum omnis generis, carminum, epistolarum, diplomatum, epitaphiorum, etc.*, ed. Jean Mabillon (Paris: Montalant, 1723; reprinted, Farnborough, Hants.: Gregg Press, 1967), 382–3.

"Adelmanni scholastici rythmi alphabetici de viris illustribus sui temporis," in *Veterum Brixiae episcoporum S. Philastrii et S. Gaudentii opera, nec non B. Ramperti, & Vener. Adelmanni opuscula*, ed. Paulus Galeardus (Brixen: ex typographia Joannis Mariae Rizzardi, 1738), 425–6.

Rerum Gallicarum et Francicarum scriptores/Receuil des historiens des Gaules et de la France, 24 vols. (Paris: aux dépens des libraires associés, 1738–1904), 11:438–9 [reprint of Mabillon's edition].

Adelmanni Brixiae episcopi de veritate corporis et sanguinis domini ad Berengarium epistola, nunc primum e codice Guelpherbytano emendata et vltra tertiam partem suppleta, cum epistola Berengarii ad Adelmannum et variis scriptis ad Adelmannum pertinentibus, ed. Conrad Arnold Schmidt (Brunswick: Typis officinae librariae orphanotrophei, 1770), 105–11.

"Adelmanni ex scholasctico Leodiensi episcopi Brixiensis Rythmi alphabetici de viris illustribus sui temporis," in *Patrologia latina, cursus completus*, ed. Jacques-Paul Migne, 221 vols. (Paris: Migne, 1844–1865), 143:1295–8 [reprint of Mabillon's edition].

"Poème rythmique d'Adelman de Liège," ed. Julien Havet, *Notices et documents publiés par la Société de l'histoire de France à l'occasion du 50ᵉ anniversaire de sa foundation* (Paris: Renouard, 1884), 71–92.

"Adelman's Poem," in Loren C. MacKinney, *Bishop Fulbert and Education at the School of Chartres*, Texts and Studies in the History of Mediaeval Education 4 (Notre Dame, Ind.: Medieval Institute, 1957), 49–51 [Havet's edition with some corrections].

(5) *Letter from Meinhard to Adelmann*[1]

Sudendorf, Hans, *Registrum, oder merkwürdige Urkunden für die deutsche Geschichte*, 3 vols. (Jena: F. Fromann; Berlin: F. Duncker, 1849–1854), vol. 3, p. 48, no. 30 [partial edition].

---

[1] Not included in this book because of its jejune content: Meinhard of Bamberg apologizes for not having congratulated Adelmann on his elevation to the bishopric and praises Adelmann's nephew.

"M[einhard] an Bischof A[delmann] von Brescia," in *Briefsammlungen der Zeit Heinrichs IV.*, ed. Carl Erdmann and Norbert Fickermann, Monumenta Germaniae historica, Die Briefe der Deutschen Kaiserzeit 5 (Weimar: H. Böhlau, 1950), 125–6.

Secondary Literature

Andreas, Valerius, *Bibliotheca belgica* (Louvain: J. Zegers, 1643), 5 [reprinted in the series Monumenta humanistica belgica 5 (Nieuwkoop: De Graaf, 1973)].

Auctoritas und Ratio. Studien zu Berengar von Tours, ed. Peter Ganz, R. B. C. Huygens, and Friedrich Niewöhner, Wolfenbütteler Mittelalter-Studien 2 (Wiesbaden: Harrassowitz, 1990).

Balau, Sylvain, *Les sources de l'histoire de Liège au moyen âge. Étude critique* (Brussels: H. Lamertin, 1903), 157–62.

Bayer, Hans, "Fingierte häretische Brief- und Propagandaliteratur der Stauferzeit: Der Briefwechsel zwischen Hugo von Honau, Peter von Wien und Hugo Etherianus—'Metamorphisis Goliae'—Epistula Adelmanns an Berengar—Briefe Thomas Becketts an Konrad von Wittelsbach—'Raptor mei pilei,'" *Sacris erudiri* 36 (1996): 161–232.

de Becdelièvre, Antoine-Gabriel, *Biographie liégeoise ou Précis historique et chronologique de toutes les personnes qui se sont rendues célèbres par leurs talents, leurs vertus ou leurs actions, dans l'ancien diocèse et pays de Liége, les duchés de Limbourg et de Bouillon, le pays de Stavelot, et la ville de Maestricht, depuis les temps les plus réculés jusqu'à nos jours*, 2 vols. (Liège: Jeunehomme, 1836–1837; reprinted, Geneva: Slatkine, 1971), 1:39 and 51.

Berlière, Ursmer, "Adelman," *Dictionnaire d'histoire et de géographie ecclésiastiques*, vol. 1 (Paris: Letouzey et Ané, 1912), 530.

Bonitho, "Bonithonis episcopi Sutrini liber ad amicum," in *Bibliotheca rerum germanicarum*, ed. Philipp Jaffé, 6 vols. (Berlin: Weidmann, 1864–1873), 2:577–689, esp. 643–4.

Brittner, Albert, *Wazo und die Schulen von Lüttich* (Breslau: Genossenschafts-Buchdruckerei, 1879) [diss. University of Breslau, 1879].

Bullough, Donald A., "Le scuole cattedrali e la cultura dell'Italia settentrionale prima dei Comuni," in *Vescovi e diocesi in Italia nel Medioevo (sec. IX–XIII). Atti del II convegno di storia della chiesa in Talia (Roma, 5–9 sett. 1961)*, Italia Sacra: Studi e documenti di storia ecclesiactica 5 (Padua: Antenore, 1964), 111–43, esp. 140 n. 3.

Calogera, Angelo, "De Adelmanni Brixiani episcopi emortuali anno atque vindiciis N.N. sacerdotis Brixiani ad concivem suum epistola," *Raccolta d'opuscoli scientifici e filologici* 47 (1752): i–xvi.

Capitani, Ovidio, "Studi per Berengario di Tours," *Bullettino dell'Istituto storico italiano per il medio evo e Archivo Muratoriano* 69 (1957): 67–173, esp. 103–11.

—, "Adelmanno," in *Dizionario biografico degli Italiani*, 65 vols. (Rome: Istituto della Enciclopedia Italiana, 1960–1982), 1, 263–5.

Cappuyns, Maïeul, "Bérenger de Tours," *Dictionnaire d'histoire et de géographie ecclésiastiques*, vol. 8 (Paris: Letouzey et Ané, 1935), 385–407.

Caspers, Charles, *De eucharistische vroomheid en het feest van Sacramentsdag in de Nederlanden tijdens de late middeleeuwen*, Miscellanea Neerlandica 5 (Louvain: Peeters, 1992), esp. 12, 26, and 45.

Ceillier, Remy, *Histoire générale des auteurs sacrés et ecclésiastiques*, 23 vols. (Paris: François Barrois et al., 1729–1763), 12:254–8.

Clerval, Jules Alexandre, *Les écoles de Chartres au moyen âge du Ve au XVIe siècle* (Paris: Picard, 1895; reprinted, Geneva: Slatkine, 1977), 34–5, 40, and 50–140.

Delarc, Odon, *Saint Grégoire VII et la réforme de l'Église au XIe siècle*, 3 vols. (Paris: Retaux-Bray, 1889), 1:203 and 212–14; 2:120 n. 1.

Dute, August, *Die Schulen im Bistum Lüttich im 11. Jahrhundert* (Marburg: Koch, 1882).

Egbertus Leodiensis, *Fecunda ratis*, ed. Ernst Voigt (Halle/Saale: Niemeyer, 1889), xxxiv–xxxviii.

Erdmann, Carl, *Studien zur Briefliteratur Deutschlands im 11. Jahrhundert*, Monumenta Germaniae historica, Schriften 1 (Leipzig: Hiersemann, 1938).

—, and Norbert Fickermann, *Briefsammlungen der Zeit Heinrichs IV.*, Monumenta Germaniae historica, Die Briefe der deutschen Kaiserzeit 5 (Weimar: Böhlau, 1950).

Galeardus, Paulus, *Veterum Brixiae episcoporum S. Philastrii et S. Gaudentii opera, nec non B. Ramperti, & Vener. Adelmanni opuscula* (Brixen: ex typographia Joannis Mariae Rizzardi, 1738), 409–12 ("Testimonia de Adelmanno").

Geiselmann, Josef Rupert, *Die Eucharistielehre der Vorscholastik*, Forschungen zur christlichen Literatur- und Dogmengeschichte 15 (Paderborn: Schöningh, 1926), 303–05.

Gorissen, Pieter, "Adelman de Liège (†1061) et le problème du wallon ancien," *Le moyen âge: Revue d'histoire et de philologie* 69 (1963): 151–6.

Gundecharus, "Gundechari Liber pontificalis Eichstetensis," in *Chronica et gesta aevi Salici*, ed. Georg Heinrich Pertz et al., Monumenta Germaniae historica, Scriptores 7 (Hanover: Hahnsche Buchhandlung, 1846), 239–52, esp. 249.

Hampe, Karl, "Reise nach England vom Juli 1895 bis Februar 1896, II.," *Neues Archiv der Gesellschaft für ältere deutsche Geschichtskunde zur Beförderung einer Gesammtausgabe der Quellenschriften deutscher Geschichten des Mittelalters* 22 (1897): 335–415, esp. 373–87: "Zur Geschichte des Bisthums Lüttich im 11. und 12. Jahrhundert."

Hauck, Albert, "Adelmann," in *Realencyclopädie für protestantische Theologie und Kirche*, ed. Albert Hauck, 3rd ed., 24 vols. (Leipzig: Hinrichs, 1896–1913), 1:167.

—, *Kirchengeschichte Deutschlands*, 8th ed., 6 vols. (Berlin: Akademie-Verlag, 1957), 3:954.

Hauréau, Barthélemy, "Mémoire sur quelques chanceliers de l'église de Chartres," *Mémoires de l'Académie des Inscriptions et Belles-Lettres* 31/2 (1880): 63–122, esp. 65 n. 1.

Havet, Julien, "Poème rythmique d'Adelman de Liège," *Notices et documents publiés par la Société de l'histoire de France à l'occasion du 50ᵉ anniversaire de sa foundation* (Paris: Renouard, 1884), 71–92.

Heurtevent, Raoul, *Durand de Troarn et les origines de l'hérésie bérengarienne*, Études de théologie historique 5 (Paris: Beauchesne, 1912).

Hocquard, Gaston, "Adelman," in *Catholicisme. Hier—Aujourd'hui—Demain. Encyclopédie*, ed. Gabriel Jacquemet, 15 vols. (Paris: Letouzey & Ané, 1948–2000), 1:138.

Kehr, Paul Fridolin, *Italia pontificia sive repertorium privilegiorum et litterarum a romanis pontificibus ante annum MCLXXXXVIII Italiae ecclesiis, monasteriis, civitatibus singulisque personis concessorum*, 11 vols. (Berlin: Weidemann, 1906–1975), 6:307–55.

Kupper, Jean-Louis, *Liège et l'Église impériale (XIᵉ-XIIᵉ siècles)*, Bibliothèque de la Faculté de philosophie et lettres de l'Université de Liège 228 (Paris: Les Belles Lettres, 1981), 379–80, 385 n.8.

Laudage, Johannes, "Adelmann von Lüttich," in *Lexikon für Theologie und Kirche*, 3rd ed., 11 vols. (Freiburg: Herder, 1993–2001), 1:154.

Lehmann, Paul, "Adelmann von Lüttich," in *Neue Deutsche Biographie* (Berlin: Duncker und Humblot, 1953–), 1:60.

Lesne, Émile, *Histoire de la propriété ecclésiastique en France*, vol. 5: *Les écoles de la fin du VIIIᵉ siècle à la fin du XIIᵉ*, Mémoires et travaux publiés par des professeurs des Facultés catholiques de Lille 50 (Lille: Facultés catholiques, 1940), 145, 153–6, 176, 199, 355–7, 361, 384, 448, 460 n. 3, 484, 506, 514, 521, 548, 557, 589, 596, 689.

Lessing, Gotthold Ephraim, *"Berengarius Turonensis," oder Ankündigung eines wichtigen Werkes desselben, wovon in der herzoglichen Bibliothek zu Wolfenbüttel ein*

    Manuscript befindlich, welches bisher völlig unerkannt geblieben (Braunschweig: Buchhandlung des Waisenhauses, 1770), 3 [Lessing's opinion on Adelmann].

Libelli de lite imperatorum et pontificum saeculis XI et XII conscripti, ed. Ernst Dümmler et al., Monumenta Germaniae Historica, Libelli de lite 1 (Hanover: Hahnsche Buchhandlung, 1891), 593.

Lubac, Henri de, *Catholicisme. Les aspects sociaux du dogme*, Unam Sanctam 3 (Paris: Cerf, 1938); republished in *Œuvres completes*, vol. 7 (Paris: Cerf, 2003).

—, *Corpus mysticum. L'eucharistie et l'Église au moyen âge*, Théologie 3 (Paris: Cerf, 1949).

Macdonald, Allan John, *Berengar and the Reform of Sacramental Doctrine* (London: Longmans, Green, 1930; reprinted, Merrick, N.Y.: Richwood, 1977), 13–16, 49–51, 121–2, 254–5, 266–71, 331.

MacKinney, Loren Carey, *Bishop Fulbert and Education at the School of Chartres*, Texts and Studies in the History of Mediaeval Education 4 (Notre Dame, Ind.: Medieval Institute, 1957).

Manitius, Max, *Geschichte der lateinischen Literatur des Mittelalters*, 3 vols. (Munich: Beck, 1911–1931; reprinted, 1964–1965), 2:558–61

de Montclos, Jean, *Lanfranc et Bérenger. La controverse eucharistique du XIe siècle*, Spicilegium sacrum Lovaniense. Études et documents 37 (Louvain: Peeters, 1971).

de Moreau, Édouard, *Histoire de l'Église en Belgique*, vol. 2: *Des origines aux débuts du XIIe siècle*, Museum Lessianum, Section historique 2 (Brussels: Édition universelle, 1940), 18–19.

d'Onofrio, Giulio, "La crisi dell'equilibrio teologico altomedievale (1030–1095)," in *Storia della teologia nel medioevo*, vol. 1: *I principi*, ed. Giulio d'Onofrio (Casale Monferrato: Piemme, 1996), 435–80, esp. 447, 451, 477.

Polman, Pontianus, *L'élément historique dans la controverse religieuse au XVIe siècle* (Gembloux: Duculot, 1932).

Potthast, August, *Repertorium fontium historiae Medii Aevi*, 11 vols. (Rome: Istituto storico italiano per il medio evo, 1962–2007), 2:123–4.

Raby, Frederic James Edward, *A History of Secular Latin Poetry in the Middle Ages*, 2nd ed. (Oxford: Clarendon, 1967), 308.

Radding, Charles M., and Francis Newton, *Theology, Rhetoric, and Politics in the Eucharistic Controversy, 1078–1079: Alberic of Monte Cassino against Berengar of Tours* (New York: Columbia University Press, 2003), 8–16.

Ramirez, Luis Carlos, *La controversia eucarística del siglo IX. Berengario de Tours a la luz de sus contemporáneos* (Rome: Università Pontificia Gregoriana, 1938).

Rivet de la Grange, Antoine, *Histoire littéraire de la France*, vol. 7 (Paris: Firmin Didot/Treuttel et Wurtz, 1746), 542–53 [Migne copied this edition for his

Patrologia latina, cursus completus, ed. Jacques-Paul Migne, 221 vols. (Paris: Migne, 1844–1865), 143:1279–87].

Rousseau, Félix, *La Meuse et le pays mosan en Belgique. Leur importance avant le XIIIe siècle* (Brussels: Culture et civilisation, 1977).

Saint-Genois, Baron Jules de, "Adelman," in *Biographie nationale publiée par l'Académie royale des sciences, des lettres et des beaux-arts de Belgique*, vol. 1 (Brussels: H. Thiry-Van Buggenhoudt, 1866), 62–3.

Schmidt, Martin Anton, "Adelmann," in *Die Religion in Geschichte und Gegenwart. Handwörterbuch in gemeinverständlicher Darstellung*, ed. Kurt Galling et al., 3rd ed., 7 vols. (Tübingen: Mohr-Siebeck Verlag, 1956–1965), 1:92.

Schnitzer, Joseph, *Berengar von Tours, sein Leben und seine Lehre. Ein Beitrag zur Abendmahlslehre des beginnenden Mittelalters* (Munich: Stahl, 1890), 318–24.

Sheedy, Charles E., *The Eucharistic Controversy of the Eleventh Century against the Background of Pre-Scholastic Theology*, Studies in Sacred Theology, 2nd Series 4 (Washington, D.C.: Catholic University of America Press, 1947; reprinted, New York: AMS, 1980).

Sigebert of Gembloux, "Liber de scriptoribus ecclesiasticis," in *Patrologia latina, cursus completus*, ed. Jacques-Paul Migne, 221 vols. (Paris: Migne, 1844–1865), 160:547–88, esp. 582.

Silvestre, Hubert, *Le "Chronicon Sancti Laurentii Leodiensis" dit de Rupert de Deutz*, Recueil de travaux d'histoire et de philologie, 3e série, 43 (Louvain: Publications universitaires, 1952), 228–31 and 264–5.

—, "Notice sur Adelman de Liège, évêque de Brescia (†1061)," *Revue d'histoire ecclésiastique* 56 (1961): 855–71.

—, "Quelle était la langue maternelle d'Adelman de Liège, évêque de Brescia (†1061)," *La vie wallonne* 36 (1962): 43–9.

—, "Adelman," *Biographie nationale publiée par l'Académie royale des sciences, des lettres et des beaux-arts de Belgique*, vol. 33: *Supplément* (Brussels: Bruylant, 1965), 1–8.

—, "Notes sur l'édition de l'épître de Bérenger de Tours à Adelman de Liège," *Recherches de théologie ancienne et médiévale* 49 (1972): 127–30.

—, "La prison de l'âme (Phédon, 62b). Nouveaux témoignages du moyen âge latin," *Latomus* 38 (1979): 982–6.

Steindorff, Ernst, *Jahrbücher des deutschen Reiches unter Heinrich III.*, 2 vols. (Leipzig: Duncker und Humblot, 1874–1881), 2:299 n. 5.

Tannery, Paul, and Jules Alexandre Clerval, "Une correspondance d'écolâtres du onzième siècle," *Notices et extraits des manuscrits de la Bibliothèque nationale et autres bibliothèques* 36 (1899): 487–543; reprinted in Paul Tannery, *Mémoires scientifiques*, ed. J.-L. Heiberg and H.-G. Zeuthen, 17 vols. (Toulouse: Privat, 1912–1950), 5:103–11.

Tegels, A. H., "Adelmannus (Almannus)," in *New Catholic Encyclopedia*, 15 vols. (San Francisco: McGraw-Hill, 1967), 1:127.

Textus antiqui de festo Corporis Christi, ed. Peter Browe, Opuscula et textus historiam Ecclesiae eiusque vitam atque doctrinam illustrantia, series liturgica 4 (Münster: Aschendorff, 1934), esp. 21.

Trithemius, Johannes, *De scriptoribus ecclesiasticis* (Basle: Johannes Amerbach, 1494), 49v [many later editions].

Ughelli, Ferdinando, *Italia sacra*, 10 vols. (Venice: Sebastianus Coleti, 1717–1722; reprinted, Bologna: Forni, 1972–1985), 4:540.

Van Sluis, Jacob, "Adelman van Luik. De eerste opponent van Berengarius van Tours," *Nederlands theologisch tijdschrift* 47 (1993): 89–106.

Wattenbach, Wilhelm, *Deutschlands Geschichtsquellen im Mittelalter. Deutsche Kaiserzeit*, ed. Robert Holtzmann, 4 vols. (Berlin: Ebering, 1938–1943), esp. vol. 1.

Wattenbach, Wilhelm, and Franz-Josef Schmale, *Deutschlands Geschichtsquellen im Mittelalter*, vol. 1: *Vom Tode Kaiser Heinrichs V. bis zum Ende des Interregnum* (Darmstadt: Wissenschaftliche Buchgesellschaft, 1976), 145–6.

Werner, Karl, "Adelmann von Brixen," in *Allgemeine Deutsche Biographie*, 56 vols. (Leipzig: Duncker und Humblot, 1875–1912), 1:78–9.

Ziezulewicz, William, "The School of Chartres and Reform Influences before the Pontificate of Leo IX," *Catholic Historical Review* 77 (1991): 383–402.

Ziezulewicz, William, "Sources of Reform in the Episcopate of Airard of Nantes (1050–1054)," *Journal of Ecclesiastical History* 47 (1996): 432–45.

Biblical References

Old Testament

Genesis
1:3	69 n. 36
19:26	91 n. 16
2:24	81 n. 114

Exodus
7:10	91 n. 16

Leviticus
14:11ff.	99 n. 8

Numbers
5:2	99 n. 7
21:22	63 n. 3

Deuteronomy
19:15	67 n. 33

Psalms
3	87
13	63
13:3	63 n. 10
18:6	81 n. 112
32:9	69 n. 35
44:10	81 n. 113
50:6	97 n. 3
81:6	97 n. 6
109:4	71 n. 52
113:3	77 n. 81
115:11	67 n. 20
118:32	63 n. 7
118:59	63 n. 11
118:165	63 n. 6
125:5	81 n. 115
134:6	77 n. 81
137:1	77 n. 87
139:6	63 n. 5
140:9	63 n. 4
148:5	69 n. 35

Proverbs
10:7	65 n. 19

Ecclesiastes
9:3	63 n. 4

Song of Solomon
1:11	83 n. 117

Isaiah
45:16	65 n. 18

Jeremiah
6:27	99 n. 15

Ezekiel
13:19	99 n. 14

Baruch
3:27	67 n. 25

Daniel
2:31–36	81 n. 107
3:87	67 n. 27
7:1	73 n. 67

Habakkuk
2:4	77 n. 82
2:19	73 n. 64

Zechariah
8:19	65 n. 5

New Testament

Matthew
7:14	83 n. 123
8:11	81 n. 110
9:6	99 n. 10
10:1	101 n. 24

11:25	67 n. 28	6:51	91 n. 18
17	29 n. 84	6:51–52	67 n. 31
18:6	85 n. 127	6:54	26
18:8–9	83 n. 125	11:1–44	99 n. 17
18:15–17	97 n. 5	12:24–25	79 n. 105
18:16	67 n. 33	14:6	67 n. 29
18:18	97 n. 4 n. 5	14:25	69 n. 48
23:13	101 n. 23	14:31	71 n. 57
26:26	89 n. 10 n. 13, 91 n.17	15:5	69 n. 39, 79 n. 104
27:52	81 n. 109	20	29 n. 84
28:20	69 n. 40, 101 n. 25	20:29	77 n. 83

Mark		Acts	
2:3–5	99 n. 12	9:4	69 n.42
2:5	99 n. 11	16:20	65 n. 16
2:7	97 n. 2	17:24	67 n. 21
2:10	99 n. 10		
3:29	101 n. 19	Romans	
14:22	89 n. 10 n. 13, 91 n. 17	1:17	77 n. 82
		1:22	67 n. 24
Luke		3:2	101 n. 21
1:18–20	75 n. 77	4:5	101 n. 20
1:78	85 n. 129	4:9–12	67 n. 34
5:21	97 n. 2	5:20	85 n. 128
5:24	99 n. 10	7:24–25	73 n. 65 n. 66
9:1–2	101 n. 24	8:23	81 n. 116
9:26	89 n. 12	8:24	71 n. 61
10:21	67 n.28	8:34	71 n. 55
10:30–34	77 n. 84	11:34	77 n. 80
16:1–8	101 n. 22		
16:2	101 n. 26	1 Corinthians	
18:13	103 n. 28	2:14	73 n. 63
22:19	71 n. 56, 89 n. 10 n. 13, 91 n. 17	3:7	5 n. 4
		5:6	77 n. 88
24	29 n. 84	6:15	79 n. 90
		9:1	69 n. 44
John		10:16	89 n. 11 n. 14, 91 n. 19
1:12	71 n.54	11:22	65 n. 12
1:33	71 n. 50 n. 53	11:24	71 n. 56, 89 n. 10 n. 13, 91 n. 17
2:1–11	69 n. 37		
2:1–12	91 n. 16	11:29	79 n. 89
3:5	73 n. 70	12:26	79 n. 103
3:10	75 n. 78	15:8	69 n. 43
3:13	69 n. 41	15:10	81 n. 106
5:2–9	99 n. 13	15:24	83 n. 120
5:25	69 n. 49	15:28	83 n. 122
5:28–29	69 n. 47	1 Cor. 15:54	83 n.119

Biblical References

2 Corinthians	
5:7	29, 44, 71 n. 58
7:5	67 n. 30
10:5	75 n.71
10:13.15	81 n. 108
12:2	69 n. 45
12:7	79 n. 100
12:12	79 n. 91
13:3	71 n. 51
13:11	67 n. 33

Galatians	
3:11	77 n. 82
5:9	77 n. 88

Ephesians	
2:5–6	79 n. 99
2:6	79 n. 101
4:13	79 n. 92
4:17	79 n. 96
5:27	83 n. 121
5:32	93 n. 25

Philippians	
1:23	81 n. 111
3:20	79 n. 98
4:7	85 n. 131

Colossians	
1:18	79 n. 95
1:24	79 n. 97
2:3	79 n. 93
2:9	79 n. 94
3:4	83 n. 118

1 Thessalonians	
4:16	69 n. 46

2 Thessalonians	
2:5	69 n. 38

1 Timothy	
2:5	75 n. 73

2 Timothy	
3:12	83 n. 124

Titus	
3:5	71 n. 62

Hebrews	
5:6	71 n. 52
7:17.21	71 n. 52
10:38	77 n. 82
11:1	29, 44, 71 n. 59
11:1–40	75 n. 76

James	
2:20	71 n. 60

1 Peter	
3:10	83 n. 126

1 John	
2:15	67 n. 21

Apocalypse	
3:7	101 n. 23
5:1	67 n. 30
12:6	65 n. 13

Index of Pre-Modern Names

Adam, 26 n. 72
Adelmann of Liège, passim
Agnes, Saint, 50
Alberic of Monte Cassino, 3
Alcuin, 24
Alestanus, 109, 115
Alger of Liège, 3, 6, 7, 9, 10, 11, 16, 17–35, 45
Amalarius of Metz, 24 n. 62
Ambrose, Saint, 4, 9, 23, 24, 48, 65, 87
Amos, 25 n. 69
Augustine, Saint, 5, 6, 8, 9, 10, 11, 12, 13, 14, 17, 19 n. 40, 20, 21, 22, 24, 26, 27, 28, 29 n. 88, 33, 35, 41, 45, 47, 48, 65, 77, 87, 93
Aulus mannus (=Adelmann), vi, 46, 105

Bede, 24
Berengar of Tours, passim
Bernard of Clairvaux, Saint, 1
Boethius, 50, 83

Catharine, Saint, 50
Cicero, 24, 50, 75
Claudianus, 50

Donatus, 83
Durandus of Troarn, 24 n. 62, 124 n. 15

Edward I, king of England, 21
Engelbert (Master), 107, 113

Fulbert of Chartres, 24 n. 62, 37, 38, 43, 45, 51, 65, 105, 107, 111, 117 n. 1, 123 n. 1 n. 3 n. 4

Gerard Gilbert (Master), 107, 113, 115
Gerardus, *see* Warinus
Gerbernus of Burgundy, 113
Gozechinus (Master in Liège), 38
Gratian, 9

Gregory the Great, Saint, 19, 21, 24, 30, 99, 117 n. 17
Guitmond of Aversa, 9, 10 n. 18, 29

Henry I, king of France, 7 n. 10, 39 n. 13
Hermann II, bishop of Cologne, 3, 39, 49, 52, 97
Herod, 8
Hilary of Poitiers, Saint, 24
Hildegerus (Master at Chartres), 105, 111, 123 n. 2
Hincmar, 24 n. 62
Hippocrates, 107, 111
Horace, 46
Hugo (son of King Robert I of France), 123 n. 5

Innocent I, pope, 24, 25 n. 66
Isidore of Seville, 5, 6, 35, 48
Ivo of Chartres, Saint, 6

Jerome, Saint, 17 n. 35, 25 n. 69, 27, 65
John the Baptist, Saint, 69, 75
John, Saint (apostle), 99
Judas, 87
Juliana of Mont-Cornillon, Saint, 2, 3

Lambert of Saint-Laurence, 38, 107, 113
Lanfranc of Bec, 2, 6, 9, 10, 21, 27 n. 75, 30, 33 n. 105, 89, 95
Lot, 91

Martinus of Tours, 107, 113, 123 n. 4
Mary Magdalene, Saint, 29
Maximus Confessor, Saint, 8
Moses, 49, 91

Naaman, 22 n. 52
Nebuchadnezzar, 81
Nicholas of Liège, 34
Notker, 123 n. 9

Odulfus (Master), 109, 115

Paul, Saint (apostle), 44, 69, 79, 91
Paschasius Radbertus, 2, 6, 19, 21, 24, 33 n. 106, 41, 45, 89, 95
Paulinus (*primicerius* of Metz), 38, 41, 42, 65
Pelagius, 19
Peter, Saint (apostle), 79
Peter Abelard, 6, 11, 33 n. 106, 35
Peter the Chanter, 21 n. 49
Peter Lombard, 2, 11,12, 29, 30, 35
Plato, 63
Priscian, 83
Prosper of Aquitane, 10 n. 20, 13
Pythagoras, 107, 111

Quintilian, 24

Radulphus (cleric at Orléans), 111, 124 n. 13
Rainald of Tours, 107, 124 n. 4
Ratramnus of Corbie, 2, 6, 14
Regimbald of Aachen, 107/109
Reginard, bishop of Liège, 37, 52
Reinbald of Aachen, 113

Reinbald of Tours, 113
Robert I, king of France, 123 n. 5
Robert of Thourotte, 2

Sallust, 24
Saul, *see* Paul
Sergius, pope (apocryphal citation), 14
Sigebert of Gembloux, 37
Sigo (cleric at Chartres), 107, 123 n. 3
Socrates, 63, 107, 111

Theoduin of Liège, 7 n. 10, 39 n. 13
Thomas Aquinas, Saint, 1, 2, 31

Urban IV, pope, 1

Virgil, 24

Walter of Burgundy, 107, 122 n. 8
Warinus (wealthy individual from Metz), 109, 122 n. 11
Wazo of Liège, 38, 109, 122 n. 9
William of Saint-Arnoul, 38
William of Saint-Thierry, 1